CONTENTS

CHRONOLOGICAL LIST OF WITNESSES

Death Benefits and Services Available to Survivors of Military Personnel and Legislative Proposals to Enhance These Benefits

FEBRUARY 1, 2005

S. Hrg. 109–296

DEATH BENEFITS AND SERVICES AVAILABLE TO SURVIVORS OF MILITARY PERSONNEL AND LEGISLATIVE PROPOSALS TO ENHANCE THESE BENEFITS

HEARING

BEFORE THE

COMMITTEE ON ARMED SERVICES UNITED STATES SENATE

ONE HUNDRED NINTH CONGRESS

FIRST SESSION

FEBRUARY 1, 2005

Printed for the use of the Committee on Armed Services

U.S. GOVERNMENT PRINTING OFFICE

26–313 PDF WASHINGTON : 2006

For sale by the Superintendent of Documents, U.S. Government Printing Office
Internet: bookstore.gpo.gov Phone: toll free (866) 512–1800; DC area (202) 512–1800
Fax: (202) 512–2250 Mail: Stop SSOP, Washington, DC 20402–0001

COMMITTEE ON ARMED SERVICES

JOHN WARNER, Virginia, *Chairman*

JOHN McCAIN, Arizona	CARL LEVIN, Michigan
JAMES M. INHOFE, Oklahoma	EDWARD M. KENNEDY, Massachusetts
PAT ROBERTS, Kansas	ROBERT C. BYRD, West Virginia
JEFF SESSIONS, Alabama	JOSEPH I. LIEBERMAN, Connecticut
SUSAN M. COLLINS, Maine	JACK REED, Rhode Island
JOHN ENSIGN, Nevada	DANIEL K. AKAKA, Hawaii
JAMES M. TALENT, Missouri	BILL NELSON, Florida
SAXBY CHAMBLISS, Georgia	E. BENJAMIN NELSON, Nebraska
LINDSEY O. GRAHAM, South Carolina	MARK DAYTON, Minnesota
ELIZABETH DOLE, North Carolina	EVAN BAYH, Indiana
JOHN CORNYN, Texas	HILLARY RODHAM CLINTON, New York
JOHN THUNE, South Dakota	

JUDITH A. ANSLEY, *Staff Director*
RICHARD D. DEBOBES, *Democratic Staff Director*

DEATH BENEFITS AND SERVICES AVAILABLE TO SURVIVORS OF MILITARY PERSONNEL AND LEGISLATIVE PROPOSALS TO ENHANCE THESE BENEFITS

TUESDAY, FEBRUARY 1, 2005

U.S. SENATE,
COMMITTEE ON ARMED SERVICES,
Washington, DC.

The committee met, pursuant to notice, at 9:39 a.m., in room SH–216, Hart Senate Office Building, Senator John Warner (chairman) presiding.

Committee members present: Senators Warner, McCain, Inhofe, Sessions, Collins, Talent, Chambliss, Graham, Dole, Cornyn, Thune, Levin, Lieberman, Akaka, Bill Nelson, E. Benjamin Nelson, Dayton, and Clinton.

Also present: Senators Allen and DeWine.

Committee staff members present: Judith A. Ansley, staff director; and Cindy Pearson, assistant chief clerk and security manager.

Majority staff members present: Gregory T. Kiley, professional staff member; Scott W. Stucky, general counsel; Diana G. Tabler, professional staff member; and Richard F. Walsh, counsel.

Minority staff members present: Richard D. DeBobes, Democratic staff director; Gabriella Eisen, research assistant; Gerald J. Leeling, minority counsel; Peter K. Levine, minority counsel; and Michael J. McCord, professional staff member.

Staff assistants present: Catherine E. Sendak, Bridget E. Ward, and Pendred K. Wilson.

Committee members' assistants present: Cord Sterling, assistant to Senator Warner; Christopher J. Paul and Marshall A. Salter, assistants to Senator McCain; John A. Bonsell, assistant to Senator Inhofe; Arch Galloway II, assistant to Senator Sessions; Lindsey R. Neas, assistant to Senator Talent; Clyde A. Taylor IV, assistant to Senator Chambliss; Meredith Moseley, assistant to Senator Graham; Christine O. Hill, assistant to Senator Dole; Mieke Y. Eoyang, assistant to Senator Kennedy; Erik Raven, assistant to Senator Byrd; Davelyn Noelani Kalipi and Darcie Tokioka, assistants to Senator Akaka; Amy Akiyama, assistant to Senator Bill Nelson; Eric Pierce, assistant to Senator Ben Nelson; and Andrew Shapiro; assistant to Senator Clinton.

OPENING STATEMENT OF SENATOR JOHN WARNER, CHAIRMAN

Chairman WARNER. The hearing will come to order. We welcome all present here today.

The world witnessed an extraordinary chapter in the history of mankind with these elections this weekend, striking a blow for freedom in Iraq. Our President, President Bush, addressed the Nation shortly after the elections were underway there on Sunday morning, and he gave due credit to all of those who made this election possible. But the courage of the men and women of the Armed Forces of the United States and other coalition forces, together with the Iraqi professional military forces and the people of Iraq and many others, are owed a great debt of gratitude. We gather here this morning to examine, in the context of a Senate hearing, the importance of giving greater recognition to the sacrifices of those who lose their lives in this cause of freedom.

I particularly welcome this morning the families who are present, the Gold Star Mothers, the National Military Family Association, and others. We thank you very much for joining us here today and not only today, but you are ever-present in your mission on behalf of the families. So it is not just today but it is 365 days a year, and we thank you very much for that.

This morning's witnesses are Dr. Chu, Under Secretary of Defense for Personnel and Readiness; General Cody, Vice Chief of Staff, United States Army; Admiral Nathman, Vice Chief of Naval Operations; General Nyland, assistant Commandant of the Marine Corps; General Moseley, Vice Chief of Staff for the Air Force; and Mr. Epley. We thank you for joining us here this morning.

I will ask unanimous consent that I place into the record my opening statement because I feel that there are members of this committee and, indeed, in a totally bipartisan manner, other Senators who have been in the very forefront of this issue. We are privileged to have on our committee our distinguished colleague, Mr. Sessions. He teamed up with Mr. Lieberman, and at this moment, I would like to recognize Senator Sessions for a few comments.

[The prepared statement of Senator Warner follows:]

PREPARED STATEMENT BY SENATOR JOHN WARNER

The committee meets today to receive testimony on the full range of death benefits and services available to survivors of military personnel, and on legislative proposals to enhance those benefits. We currently have five such proposals referred to this committee. I thank our witnesses for being here today, and look forward to their views on this timely and important subject.

Based on news reports we began to see last night—in advance of receiving your written testimony, Mr. Secretary, this hearing would appear to be very timely. It was reported that the President has indicated he will support significant increases in death benefits, to include increasing the death gratuity to $100,000 retroactive to October 7, 2001, and raising the insurance available under Servicemembers' Group Life Insurance (SGLI) from $250,000 to $400,000. We look forward to hearing your testimony about these reports.

There is, of course, no issue of greater importance to this committee than the well-being of the families of the men and women who serve in our Armed Forces. These brave individuals who make up our superb All-Volunteer Force are able to serve, in no small measure, because of the support and encouragement of their spouses, children, parents, and other family members. Protecting the welfare of these family members—particularly the spouses and dependent children—is a sacred trust that the Services share with individual servicemembers.

By their very nature, military operations, military training, and military service involve danger and the ever-present risk of injury and fatalities. While extraordinary efforts are made throughout the force each day to ensure all personnel are fully trained and ready in every respect for the dangers that may await them, casualties are incurred. The ongoing operations in Iraq and Afghanistan have underscored these dangers, but also the strengths of the All-Volunteer Force. Our Nation owes a debt of gratitude to the men and women of the Armed Forces and their families. Our prayers go out to those who have made the ultimate sacrifice and those who have been injured in defense of freedom and for their families.

Congress and this committee, in particular, have been diligent over the years in carefully monitoring and, where necessary, enhancing the death benefits and services available to military personnel. I am proud of the committee's record in constantly working to improve programs under our jurisdiction, such as the Survivor Benefit Plan (SBP), the death gratuity, TRICARE, and various benefits that assist surviving family members of those who die in uniform. I note that there is an additional series of benefits which falls under the jurisdiction of the Veterans' Affairs Committee.

The Department of Defense (DOD) has been a full partner in the effort to ensure survivors and next of kin of military personnel are adequately provided for. Recent studies by DOD and the Government Accountability Office (GAO) concluded that the system of benefits provided to survivors of members who die on Active-Duty is "adequate, substantial, and comprehensive," but these studies provided suggestions for improvements and set the stage for the discussions we engage in today and the recommendations for change we are about to receive.

With the start of the 109th Congress, several of our colleagues have introduced legislation that would further enhance the benefits made available to survivors and next of kin of those who die on Active-Duty. For example, the Majority Leader introduced S.3, the Protecting America in the War on Terror Act of 2005, on January 24. Title II of this bill provides for an increase in the death gratuity to $100,000, raises the limit on SGLI to $300,000, and enhances the TRICARE medical coverage already available to dependent children of military decedents.

Senator Sessions has introduced the (HEROES) Act—S.77, which has provisions very similar to those reported last night. I note that Senator Lieberman is the primary co-sponsor. This legislation would raise the level of SGLI coverage to $400,000 and also increase the death gratuity to $100,000. I congratulate Senator Sessions on his leadership and untiring efforts over the past 2 years on this subject.

Our ranking member, Senator Levin, introduced S.11, which, among its various purposes, would enhance death benefits. There are others: S.44, introduced by Senators Hagel, Kennedy, and Clinton; S.121 introduced by Senator DeWine; and S.42, introduced by Senator Allen.

Clearly, this is a subject of great importance. In consultation with Senator Levin, I decided to have an early hearing on this issue. The presence here today of all of the Service Vice Chiefs, as well as the Under Secretary of Defense for Personnel and Readiness, and a representative from the Department of Veterans' Affairs (VA) will ensure a comprehensive exchange of views. My expectation is that I and the members of the committee will come away with a better understanding of the actions that need to be taken in the future.

Chairman WARNER. I'd also like to insert Senator Roberts' statement for the record at the point.

[The prepared statement of Senator Roberts follows:]

PREPARED STATEMENT BY SENATOR PAT ROBERTS

Thank you Mr. Chairman. I would like to thank our distinguished panel for being here today and for their service to the country. I know your time is valuable, and I appreciate your attention to this matter.

We are here to discuss an important responsibility borne by the Armed Services—how to assist the families of soldiers who make the ultimate sacrifice. Fort Riley, in my home State of Kansas, has sent thousands of soldiers to Iraq and Afghanistan, and will continue to send soldiers until the fight is over. Sadly, not all return. When that happens, we all share the responsibility of ensuring that family members left behind, spouses and children alike, are provided for financially. I am pleased that the administration has announced that it will increase the death gratuity as well as the amount of life insurance our service men and women will receive in the event they make the ultimate sacrifice on behalf of the Nation.

There is another issue I would like to briefly discuss. Across the Nation, civilian employers of members of the Guard and Reserve have gone above the call of duty in extending differential pay to the reservists called to serve. This differential pay ensures reservists that their families will be provided for financially while they are serving overseas. However, the Internal Revenue Service (IRS) tells employers and their deployed employees that because of an obscure revenue ruling made nearly four decades ago, the differential pay provided cannot be considered as a wage and, as a result, the servicemember who receives this pay will have to file and pay a quarterly estimated income tax or face stiff penalties. Congress found this practice absurd and adopted a resolution as part of last year's Department of Defense authorization bill which essentially told the IRS to fix this matter. The IRS, to date, has done nothing except further burden the men and women in uniform and their families. I hope you will agree with me that this situation needs to be fixed.

Gentlemen, it seems as though we must prod the IRS into providing safe harbor for guardsmen and reservists serving on Active-Duty and, at the very least, ensure that the IRS provides the necessary resources to our troops and their families so that, between fighting insurgents and rebuilding a nation, our troops can file their quarterly estimated tax returns.

I hope you all agree with me that this is an archaic ruling that helps no one, and serves only to harm the citizen soldiers who fight for freedom around the world. As we continue to explore ways to provide the very best for our soldiers and their families, I implore the Services to address this matter.

Chairman WARNER. Senator Sessions.

Senator SESSIONS. Thank you, Mr. Chairman.

As you think about it, for our Nation to be able to be effective militarily, there needs to be a bond between the people and the soldiers who go out and put their lives at risk to execute the policies that the people have asked them to execute. There needs to be a deep and abiding bond there.

In the legislation that Senator Lieberman and I have offered, I have just been really impressed with the grass roots support and the surge of support that I am seeing from the American people, because they want to be involved. They want to be sure that the families of soldiers who are serving our country and give their lives for their country are well taken care of if something happens to them. Soldiers that go and serve our country and put their lives at risk, need to know that if something happens to them, their families will be well taken care of. I think that is the bond that we are involved in here.

It is true that we have done a number of things to take care of families, and some have erroneously felt that the only benefit that families get is the death benefit of $12,000, which was increased by the leadership of Senator Collins to my left here just a few months ago or a year or so ago. That is sort of where we are. I think the opportunity we have today is to step forward as a Nation to be generous to those who have given their lives for their country, and to take care of their families in an effective way.

I want to thank Dr. Chu and the Department of Defense (DOD). After we put language in last year's National Defense Authorization Act (NDAA) asking that you review this situation and help us work to achieve it, you have come back to me and Senator Lieberman, and you presented ideas, some of which we have worked, and drafted what we call the Honoring Every Requirement of Exemplary Service (HEROES) Act, which I think fundamentally addresses the core problems, which are increased death benefits and increased Servicemembers' Group Life Insurance (SGLI). There are other ideas out there from other Senators that also deserve serious consideration and that we can move forward.

You have said you would put it in the budget. I am also pleased that the President has indicated today his support and that it would be in the budget.

So, Mr. Chairman, I will not take any more time. Thank you for giving me this opportunity to sum up where we are. I believe we have an excellent panel, people who really know their business. They know the soldiers, sailors, airmen, and marines and what their lives are like, and I look forward to that discussion as we go forward.

Chairman WARNER. Thank you very much, Senator Sessions.

Senator Lieberman, your distinguished colleague said you can proceed here on your side of the aisle for a minute.

Senator LIEBERMAN. Thanks very much, Mr. Chairman. Thanks to you and to Senator Levin for giving me this opportunity.

It has been a great honor to work with Senator Sessions and others on both sides of the aisle on this matter. As we worked together, Senator Sessions and I, on the Airland Subcommittee, we confronted the reality of the death benefits that we were providing for those who were giving their lives and risking their lives in defense of our freedom and our security. The more we knew, the more shocked and outraged we became and the more we wanted to do something about it. As we worked together, we knew that the more people learned what we had learned, the more everybody would agree we had to do something because the current situation is simply wrong and unfair, and it is in the most fundamental sense of American values, un-American.

That is how the HEROES Act came together. We have, I think, almost 20 co-sponsors from both parties.

I am very grateful to hear this morning that the President, the administration, and the Pentagon are embracing these ideas, supporting them, and most important of all putting them in the budget. That will make them real, as the witnesses will testify to today, they will be generous and retroactive to the fall of 2001 so that they will cover the survivors of all who have given their lives in the conflicts that have occurred since then.

Just to say very briefly, apart from the paltry sum of the death benefit itself, even when added to the other benefits it is not enough, particularly when compared to the appropriately generous compensation we gave to those who lost their lives on September 11. When you compare the two, there was an imbalance that is not acceptable. I believe the average award for survivors of September 11 victims was over $2 million. I understand that there are different circumstances, but still, it is a measure of America's trust and generosity to those who we lose in this and other conflicts.

The fact is, as you all know better than we, the military has changed, and when its original death benefit was set, the military was largely young, single men. Today, if I have it right, well over half those on Active-Duty are married. They have families.

Look at Iraq today. Is it 40 percent Reserve and Guard now? Maybe it is getting close to 50 percent and probably going to go down. Any of us who have been over there and seen it know our own Reserve and Guard are there. These folks are in their 30s, 40s, and 50s with families. If, God forbid, they lose their lives, we do not want their families to have to live not only with the profound pain and loss of having lost their loved one, but also in poverty. It is just not our way. That is why we are getting together in a very hopeful act, way beyond partisan lines, to make this wrong right.

There is a wonderful line that I saw from Teddy Roosevelt who said probably a century ago or more: "A man who is good enough to shed blood for his country is good enough to be given a square deal afterward." Of course, that is a compelling argument for veterans' benefits of all kinds. But, maybe in this regard, we should amend the great T.R.'s words and say that men and women good enough to risk their lives in defense of our country ought to know that if they are called upon to make the ultimate sacrifice, that they can be confident that their families will be well taken care of. That is what we all are going to join together to do today.

I thank you, Mr. Chairman, Senator Levin, and Senator Sessions, again, it is a great pleasure to work with you as always.

I thank the witnesses for the good news that they are bringing us and America's service men and women this morning. Thank you, Mr. Chairman.

Chairman WARNER. Thank you, Senator Lieberman.

Senator Allen, you and Senator Nelson put in legislation. We are glad to have you join us this morning.

STATEMENT OF SENATOR GEORGE ALLEN, U.S. SENATOR FROM THE STATE OF VIRGINIA

Senator ALLEN. Thank you, Mr. Chairman, and thank you for your leadership once again on issues that matter to those who are serving our country.

I have joined with Senator Nelson of Florida in introducing S.42.

I want to commend Senator Collins for, over the years, working on this question of death benefits or the death gratuity and Senator Sessions' measure as well which has more than just the death gratuity.

I will speak very briefly, first thanking all those families who have also made the ultimate sacrifice for the advancement of freedom. They ought to feel success and a bit of pride with the elections in Iraq because their son or their daughter, their husband, their spouse, or maybe one of their parents was involved in this effort to bring freedom to Iraq and also make our country secure.

The death gratuity, when I first saw it, was about $6,000, which seemed to be a pathetic amount. It was taxed. Senator Collins doubled it, and I was cosponsor of that, as well as many here to make it nontaxable. Still, $12,000. Someone loses their life serving our country. It is a paltry, miserly, and indeed in my view, insulting amount.

So Senator Nelson is signing on this measure, as well as Senator Dole, Mike DeWine, Ben Nelson, David Vitter, Senator Collins, and Lisa Murkowski. It is to increase the death gratuity to $100,000.

How does one determine what is an appropriate amount? It is always hard to value life, but I looked at what our law enforcement and fire fighters receive across this country if they die, and it is generally between $50,000 and $100,000. In Virginia, Mr. Chairman, the average is $75,000. $100,000 will not replace that loved one, but I think a grateful Nation, it is my sincere sense, wants to provide for those families who have also made the ultimate sacrifice.

So I am glad to hear the administration is on board. Our measure is retroactive to October 1, 2001 when the military action occurred. It simply increases the death gratuity from $12,000 to $100,000, and whether one is in a combat zone or not, if one is on duty, they will receive that death gratuity.

I thank you, Mr. Chairman, for your leadership on this and many other issues.

Chairman WARNER. Thank you, Senator Allen.

Senator ALLEN. Sorry, Mr. Chairman. I have a Foreign Relations Committee meeting right now on Iraq and will have to leave.

Chairman WARNER. Thank you very much.

Senator Bill Nelson.

Senator BILL NELSON. Thank you, Mr. Chairman, and thank you for your leadership.

We are all of one accord here in modernizing this benefit, but there is another inequity that needs to be corrected and that is how we treat our widows and orphans. Need I remind any of you it is from the Holy Scriptures. The Good Book, both in Isaiah, as well as in the New Testament in James, says there is no higher priority than the widows and orphans.

Yet, we have a glaring, unfair inequity in law that people purchase their retiree disability benefits. They are entitled to survivors' benefits. But under current law, if you happen to be the survivor, a widow or orphan, of a disabled person, of which you are entitled to those benefits too, in fact, they are offset. So we will hear testimony about how much this costs, but the fact is it is a glaring unfairness in the way that we treat widows and orphans. If one has purchased a certain benefit under survivors' benefits and are entitled to another benefit because of disability, why under current law should we allow it to stand that they offset each other?

So I am going to keep ringing the bell, Mr. Chairman, for fairness that we treat the least of these among us as they should be treated.

[The prepared statement of Senator Bill Nelson follows:]

PREPARED STATEMENT BY SENATOR BILL NELSON

Thank you, Mr. Chairman. Today I'd like to discuss two glaring inequities in how this country treats the survivors of its military retirees. It is my belief that we owe a solemn debt to those men and women who spend the best years of their lives in military service to their country, and who have dedicated themselves to preserving our freedom. Quite simply, I cannot think of a nobler life's mission.

How we treat our veterans and their families is a reflection of our esteem for their service. As one newsmagazine recently put it, "America's commitment to the survivors of the tsunami is a mark of our generosity. The commitment we make to those who voluntarily put themselves in harm's way to fight our wars is a mark of our character."

Last year, Congress and this committee made great progress to benefit military retirees and their families by repealing the law that prohibits concurrent receipt of military retired pay and Department of Veterans' Affairs (VA) disability compensation for our 100 percent disabled retirees. I have received hundreds of letters in my office from veterans living in my State of Florida, thanking this committee and Congress for treating them with the dignity that their service demands.

Mr. Chairman, despite this success, many military retirees and their survivors still face unfair treatment in receiving the benefits they have earned or purchased. The same sort of unfair benefit reduction that we just eliminated in the last Congress for 100 percent disabled retirees still exists for their survivors—between payments from the Survivors' Benefit Plan (SBP) and the VA Dependency and Indemnity Compensation (DIC). This is the first of the two inequities that are addressed in legislation that I have introduced in S.185, the Military Retiree Survivor Benefit Equity Act of 2005.

As my colleagues will know, the SBP is a purchased annuity which, after years of premium payments, provides income to the survivors of 100 percent disabled military retirees and those who die in Active service. The VA's DIC benefit is received by the surviving spouse of an Active-Duty or retired military member who dies from a service-connected cause. Under current law, even if the surviving spouse of such a servicemember is eligible for SBP, that purchased annuity is reduced by the amount of DIC she receives.

Mr. Chairman, I have conducted some research into this matter, and neither I nor my staff can find another incidence of a purchased annuity benefit being cancelled or reduced on the basis that some other source of income exists. It simply is not fair that this benefit can be taken away due to cause of death. If military service caused a retired member's death, the VA indemnity compensation should be added to the SBP the retiree paid for, not substituted for it. For members killed on Active-Duty, a surviving spouse can avoid the dollar-for-dollar offset only by assigning SBP to children. But that forfeits any SBP claim after the children reach adulthood, leaving the spouse with benefits less than $1,000 per month in DIC from the VA. Mr. Chairman, brave Americans who give their lives for their country deserve fairer treatment for those they leave behind.

Mr. Chairman, the U.S. Government gives DIC to the families of military personnel whose death is related to their service because we feel that such honorable sacrifices merit something extra. Not because we believe that the families of such men and women no longer deserve the SBP benefit they have paid for.

The Military Retiree Survivor Benefit Equity Act of 2005 addresses this situation in two important ways. First, it repeals the offset language in the law, which is the basis of the problem I have just described. Second, it allows those surviving spouses who have assigned SBP to their children to switch it back to themselves. Together these two changes to the current law will set right the treatment of surviving spouses.

The second serious problem for SBP recipients addressed in the Military Retiree Survivor Benefit Equity Act of 2005 is the effective date for paid-up status. As my colleagues know, the National Defense Authorization Act for Fiscal Year 1999 provided that SBP enrollees may stop paying premiums if they have reached 70 years of age and have been paying in for 30 years. The problem with this arrangement is that the effective date was set at October 1, 2008. The SBP program was started in 1972, meaning that there were 36 years between the effective date and when the earliest enrollees joined the system. Military enrollees who joined SBP between 1972 and 1978 are therefore required to pay for more than 30 years to reach paid-up status, whereas everyone who came after them is paid-up after just 30.

Mr. Chairman, this effective date of October 1, 2008, forces thousands of "greatest generation" retirees who signed up for SBP at its beginning to pay premiums for up to 36 years. The intention of the law is that retirees will pay into SBP for 30 years, and then reach paid-up status. The letter of the law, however, dictates that while most retirees will pay premiums for 30 years and reach paid-up status, our most aged retirees, many of them World War II combat veterans now in their eighties, will be forced to pay up to 20 percent longer. These early retirees also paid the highest premiums since they were set at 10 percent of retired pay until 1990, when they were reduced to 6.5 percent. I submit to you, Mr. Chairman, that this inequity is not what the 105th Congress had in mind when they allowed paid-up status.

The Military Retiree Survivor Benefit Equity Act of 2005 addresses this second problem very directly, by changing the effective date from October 1, 2008, to October 1, 2005. This will end the waiting now being imposed upon our most aged retirees, beginning in fiscal year 2006.

It is time to provide our military retirees and their families what they have earned and purchased, and restore basic fairness to military widows, widowers, and retirees. I call for support from my Senate colleagues for this important legislation.

Mr. Chairman, my thanks to you and Senator Levin for your leadership, to my colleagues on the Armed Services Committee for their consideration, and to the leaders of our armed services with us today. I look forward to the work we will do together as we move this important bill to final passage.

Chairman WARNER. I thank you very much, Senator. We will have the opportunity to explore those other options.

I would like to say the distinguished ranking member of the committee, Senator Levin, introduced his own legislation. Senator Levin, I would like very much to recognize your contribution in this important effort and ask now if you would like to make a complete opening statement.

STATEMENT OF SENATOR CARL LEVIN

Senator LEVIN. Thank you, Mr. Chairman. Thank you very much for holding this very important hearing.

I join you first in welcoming our impressive panel of witnesses and also a particularly warm welcome to families and those who have been fighting for fairness and equity for benefits for a long time. We will keep that fight going as long as they are here and as long as their families are here to join with them.

I hope this hearing will help the American public to understand the current benefit system and to guide us toward an enhancement of these benefits because they are simply inadequate. No benefit can replace the loss of a life of a soldier, sailor, airman, or marine who gives his or her life in service to our country. Every survivor would choose to have the servicemember alive and healthy rather than any compensation that our Government could provide. But that does not mean that our benefits should not be full and generous. To say what I just did is simply a recognition that we cannot place a monetary value on a life that is given in service to our Nation.

Yesterday, the DOD reported that over 1,400 servicemembers have given their lives in Iraq, almost 1,100 of them now in hostile action. Nearly every day, we learn about servicemembers killed in ambushes by improvised explosive devices (IEDs), helicopter crashes, including the helicopter crash last week that took the lives of 30 marines and 1 sailor. Our men and women in the military have opened the door for a democratic Iraq. They have made it possible that Iraqis now can walk through that door, and there are many steps ahead, and more of our lives, as well as Iraqi lives, of course, are going to be lost in this effort.

How does this Nation reach out to survivors of these brave servicemembers to express our gratitude and to make sure that the survivors are not left on their own to deal with the loss of their loved one who in most cases, as Senator Lierberman has pointed out, provides the primary financial support for that family?

Survivors currently receive immediate financial assistance in the form of a death gratuity, currently at $12,400. It is adjusted upward each year to keep pace with increases in military pay. That is the immediate tax-free, lump-sum payment that is supposed to help survivors cover living expenses and other immediate needs until other benefits have time to kick in. As has been indicated by everyone who has spoken and, I believe, as is felt by every member of this committee, that benefit is totally inadequate.

A number of other benefits kick in later to support the survivors. Every Active-Duty servicemember is automatically enrolled in the Government-subsidized SGLI for $250,000, unless the servicemember specifically and positively elects lesser or no coverage. Very few servicemembers opt out of the maximum coverage and that benefit is tax-free.

There are then two annuities that apply. Survivors receive Dependency and Indemnity Compensation (DIC), which is a non-taxable monthly annuity administered by the Department of Veterans' Affairs (VA). Surviving spouses also receive an annuity through the military Survivors' Benefit Plan (SBP). The amount of this annuity varies by length of service and by the rank of the servicemember. It is equal to 55 percent of the pay that the servicemember would have been entitled to on the day that he or she died, based on 100 percent disability. That is the reference that Senator Bill Nelson has made. The amount of a spouse's SBP annuity is reduced by the amount of the DIC received from the VA.

I want to repeat that because this is a huge issue. It is one that Senator Bill Nelson addresses, and I think all of us must take note of and, hopefully, correct it. The amount of a spouse's SBP annuity is reduced by the amount of the DIC which is received from the VA.

Now, a number of legislative proposals to increase these benefits have been offered by members of this committee and Members of Congress. Reacting to the pressure, the Pentagon has come around and announced yesterday that it would support an increase in the death gratuity to $100,000 and the SGLI benefit to $400,000. However, there are a number of problems with the Pentagon proposal.

First, their proposal limits the death gratuity increase to members serving in areas of operation (AOs) designated by the Secretary of Defense. The increased insurance would be paid for by the Government only for members serving in those same areas.

Now, I obviously support the increases. I think most all of us probably do, but I also believe that they should apply to survivors of all members who die on Active-Duty. The bill that was introduced by the Democratic leadership this week, called S.11, The Standing with Our Troops Act of 2005, would increase the death gratuity to $100,000 for all servicemembers who die on Active-Duty. It would eliminate the requirement that a surviving spouse's survivor benefit annuity be reduced by the amount of DIC received by the VA. Again, that is the point which Senator Bill Nelson has referred to and which he has fought to try to correct.

Now, we received, Mr. Chairman, a statement from the National Military Family Association (NMFA) that states the following: "The survivor benefit package should not create inequities by awarding different benefits to families who lose a servicemember in a hostile zone versus those who lose their loved one in a training mission preparing for service in a hostile zone. To the family, the loss is the same."

Now, that highly respected organization also states that "the benefit change that will provide the most significant long-term protection to the family's financial security would be to end the dependency and indemnity compensation offset to the survivor benefit plan." So we have to put this in front of us as one of the changes to be considered, one that I think many of us, including myself, very much support.

I want to thank that Association and the others who have come here today and all who fight and advocate for military families. I would request, Mr. Chairman, that the full statement of the National Military Family Association be included in the record at this time.

Chairman WARNER. Without objection.

[The prepared statement of the National Military Family Association follows:]

PREPARED STATEMENT BY THE NATIONAL MILITARY FAMILY ASSOCIATION

The National Military Family Association (NMFA) is the only national organization whose sole focus is the military family and whose goal is to influence the development and implementation of policies that will improve the lives of those family members. Our mission is to serve the families of the seven uniformed services through education, information and advocacy.

Founded in 1969 as the National Military Wives Association, NMFA is a non-profit 501(c)(3) primarily volunteer organization. NMFA today represents the interests of family members and the Active-Duty, National Guard, Reserve, and retired personnel of the Army, Navy, Air Force, Marine Corps, Coast Guard, Public Health Service, and the National Oceanic and Atmospheric Administration.

NMFA volunteer representatives in military communities worldwide provide a direct link between military families and NMFA's staff in the Nation's capital. Representatives are the "eyes and ears" of NMFA, bringing shared local concerns to national attention. NMFA receives no Federal grants and has no Federal contracts. NMFA's Web site is located at http://www.nmfa.org.

Mr. Chairman and distinguished members of the committee, the NMFA appreciates your interest in military families, especially the survivors of those who have made the ultimate sacrifice. NMFA is grateful for the opportunity to present testimony about the needs of those families. We believe the focus should be on the total package of benefits available for them, immediately and for the long term.

NMFA is grateful to the committee for the work it has done over the past several years to enhance the benefits provided to all survivors of those killed on Active-Duty or as a result of disabilities incurred as a result of Active-Duty service. The extension of the Survivor Benefit Plan (SBP) annuity payment to the survivors of servicemembers killed on Active-Duty is an example of those enhancements. We believe that the government's obligation as articulated by President Lincoln, "to care for him who shall have borne the battle and for his widow and his orphan," is as valid today as it was at the end of the Civil War. The committee's willingness to provide a forum for discussion of all aspects of benefits for survivors of Active-Duty deaths serves an important purpose. As seen in media reports and in questions we hear from military families and others concerned about military families, NMFA believes there is a lot of misinformation and confusion about what the complete benefit is for those whose servicemembers have made the ultimate sacrifice. We know that there is no way to compensate them for their loss, but we do owe it to these families to help ensure a secure future.

NMFA strongly believes that all servicemembers' deaths should be treated equally. Servicemembers are on duty 24 hours a day, 7 days a week, 365 days a year. Through their oath, each servicemember's commitment is the same. The survivor benefit package should not create inequities by awarding different benefits to families who lose a servicemember in a hostile zone versus those who lose their loved one in a training mission preparing for service in a hostile zone. To the family, the loss is the same.

In this testimony, NMFA will focus on the survivor benefits package as it pertains to the survivors of those killed in the line of duty while serving on Active-Duty including those eligible members of the Guard and Reserve. A summary of the Federal benefits provided to survivors is provided in Appendix 1.

CONCERNS AND RECOMMENDATIONS

A scene is becoming all too common as America wages the global war against terrorism. Brave servicemembers are sacrificing their lives in service to their country. It may happen on a dusty battlefield or village in Iraq or Afghanistan or may be the result of an unfortunate helicopter crash at Fort Hood, Texas. While specifics vary by Service, the overall process is the same. The family is visited by the casualty notification team consisting of the chaplain and a member of the servicemember's unit. This family will never be the same again. A casualty assistance officer is assigned to help the family cope with the trying days ahead. Funeral arrangements are made. The memorial service is conducted with military honors and the spouse is presented a flag on behalf of a grateful nation. The bugler blows Taps and the family goes home.

The spouse encounters a confusing array of decisions that must be made, the consequences of which will influences his or her life and the lives of the children for years to come. What can be done to alleviate the stress and confusion facing the family? What changes can be made to the present package of benefits to recognize the service and sacrifice of the servicemember and family and provide appropriate compensation that promotes the financial stability of the family?

NMFA believes the benefit change that will provide the most significant long-term protection to the family's financial security would be to end the Dependency Indemnity Compensation (DIC) offset to the SBP. The DIC is a special indemnity (compensation or insurance) payment that is paid by the Department of Veterans' Affairs (VA) to the survivor when the servicemember's service causes his or her death. It is a flat rate payment, which for 2005 is $993 for the surviving spouse and $247 for each surviving child. The SBP annuity, paid by the Department of Defense (DOD) reflects the longevity of the service of the military member. It is ordinarily calculated at 55 percent of retired pay. Military retirees who elect SBP pay a portion of their retired pay to ensure that their family has a guaranteed income should the retiree die. If that retiree dies due to a service-connected disability, their survivor is also eligible for DIC.

Two years ago, surviving spouses of all servicemembers killed on Active-Duty were made eligible to receive SBP. The amount of their annuity payment is calculated as if the servicemember was medically retired at 100 percent disability. The equation is the basic pay times 75 percent times 55 percent. As seen in the examples included at the end of this testimony (pp. 9–12), the annuity varies greatly, depending on the servicemember's longevity of service. As the law is written presently, if the amount of SBP is less than $993, the surviving spouse receives only the DIC payment of $993 per month. If the amount of SBP is greater than $993, the surviving spouse receives the DIC payment of $993 per month (which is nontaxable) plus the difference between the DIC and the SBP. For example, if the SBP is $1,500, the surviving spouse receives $993 from DIC (nontaxable) and $507 from SBP that is subject to tax each month. The DIC payment of $247 for each child is not offset.

Surviving Active-Duty spouses have the option of several benefit choices depending on their circumstances and the ages of their children. By law, the SBP benefit is awarded to the spouse. As can be seen in the examples, it is paid for the spouse's lifetime unless she remarries. Because SBP is offset by the DIC payment, the spouse whose SBP payment would be less than the amount of DIC may choose to waive her SBP benefit and select the "child only" option. In this scenario, the spouse would receive the DIC payment and her children would receive the full SBP amount until the last child turns 18 (23 if in college), as well as the individual child DIC until each child turns 18 (or 23 if in college). As shown in the examples, once the children have left the house, the spouse who has chosen this option will be left with an annual income of $11,916 (in 2005 dollars). If there are no dependent children, the surviving spouse whose SBP benefit is less than the $993 DIC payment will experience this income decline just 6 months following the servicemember's death. In each case, this is a significant drop in income from what the family had been earning while on Active-Duty. The percentage of income loss is even greater for survivors whose servicemembers had served longer on Active-Duty. Those who give their lives for their country deserve fairer compensation for their surviving spouses.

It has only been since the passage of the National Defense Authorization Act for Fiscal Year 2002 that surviving spouses of servicemembers who had not been retirement eligible and were killed on Active-Duty have been entitled to receive the SBP benefit. This eligibility was made retroactive to 10 September 2001. A correction in P.L. 108–136 allows spouses to choose "child only" SBP benefits. This change, effective only for deaths after 24 November 2003, allows some families to recover the SBP benefits the spouse would lose because of the DIC offset, but only temporarily. When the children's eligibility ends because of age, the SBP benefit is lost to the family.

As we have described, the interaction between SBP and DIC is a complex procedure to understand. Consider trying to make decisions about this payment distribution a month after losing your spouse, while still in a state of shock and denial.

NMFA recommends that the DIC offset to SBP be eliminated. Doing so would recognize the length of commitment and service of the career servicemember and spouse and would relieve the spouse of making hasty financial decisions at a time when he or she is emotionally vulnerable.

NMFA believes that the survivor benefits package, as outlined in Appendix 1, needs to be viewed as a whole and each individual benefit be studied in the context of the whole package. The recent emphasis on the death gratuity, for example, leads many of the uninformed to believe that it is the only compensation that the surviving family receives. The death gratuity, currently $12,420, is paid within 72 hours to help the families meet immediate expenses related to the death of the servicemember. NMFA applauds recent increases to the death gratuity, including the indexing of the payment to increases in basic pay. As with these previous changes, any further increase should be applied equally for all Active-Duty deaths.

NMFA recommends that any increased funding for the death gratuity be applied to increase it across-the-board for all Active-Duty deaths.

The largest payment provided to surviving families soon after the servicemember's death is from the Servicemembers' Group Life Insurance (SGLI). The maximum coverage is currently $250,000. NMFA believes the Services must educate young servicemembers on the importance of signing up for maximum coverage under SGLI and especially on updating beneficiary data. Information provided to NMFA indicates that more than 90 percent of Active-Duty servicemembers sign up for the maximum amount. The opt-out system, wherein the servicemember needs to show why he or she does not require SGLI, goes a long way in ensuring this participation. We are, however, less sure that National Guard and Reserve members are signing up at the same high rate. The election of insurance is a family decision. Spouses should be included in the decision making process and no servicemember should be allowed to opt-out without the written consent of his or her spouse. We all have heard of a few unfortunate instances where the servicemember had opted out of SGLI when first offered it, then marries and does not sign up for it. There are also cases where the servicemember does not change beneficiary or primary next of kin on the paperwork when he or she marries. While beneficiary information is supposed to be reviewed periodically, in actuality some people fall through the cracks. NMFA proposes a trigger mechanism, perhaps tied to TRICARE Defense Enrollment Eligibility Reporting System (DEERS) registration, which would prompt the servicemember to update survivor information when he or she has a change in marital status or adds a dependent.

NMFA is aware that proposals to increase the amount of SGLI are currently under discussion. We believe it is paramount that any proposal to increase the maximum SGLI should be designed to create an incentive for the servicemember to take the maximum amount. For example, NMFA supports the proposal included in the National Defense Authorization Act (NDAA) for Fiscal Year 2005, that would provide an additional $100,000 in coverage without an increase in the premium for servicemembers electing the maximum amount. Any increase in maximum coverage should be available to all servicemembers.

NMFA recommends that spouses be involved in the decision process if the servicemember elects to opt-out of SGLI. We also suggest a trigger mechanism to prompt the servicemember to update survivor information, i.e. designation of primary next of kin, election of SGLI, or change of beneficiary, when family status changes. NMFA also recommends that proposals to increase coverage be designed to ensure that the servicemember take the maximum amount and that the maximum coverage be available to all servicemembers on Active-Duty.

Much of the benefit confusion experienced by surviving families could be corrected by educating the servicemember and spouse about the total survivor benefit package. While some commanders or family readiness group leaders are reluctant to talk about this with families because they feel it will induce added stress or concern, the opposite is true. If the families have an overview of what benefits are available in case of the death of the servicemember, this knowledge can help relieve the stress when they go over the "what if" scenarios during a deployment. NMFA has a concise overview of survivor benefits in fact sheet format available on its Web site. We feel, however, that DOD should provide a more in-depth overview or explanation, like the annually-updated VA benefits, to be made available in pamphlet form and on-line to educate servicemembers and their families. The DOD booklet should focus on the survivor benefits available from all Federal sources and not get caught up in the minutiae of individual Service procedures.

NMFA recommends that DOD create a handbook similar to the annual VA Benefits Handbook to provide easy access to survivor benefit information to servicemembers and spouses.

The surviving family is presented with a large payment ($250,000 SGLI plus the $12,420 death gratuity) when the servicemember dies. The management of that large sum of money is a huge responsibility, especially if young children are involved. The surviving spouse also needs to make decisions that impact the family for many years. The bereaved spouse may be especially vulnerable to unscrupulous or uninformed advisors, friends or family members who may try to take advantage and "help" the surviving spouse spend or invest the inheritance. The need for unbiased and fair financial counseling has never been greater. At the present time, the VA offers the free services of a financial counseling service "Financial Point" for 1 year after the servicemember is killed. The access to a long term service to counsel the family members about what their options are without a financial stake in the outcome could help the surviving families establish an investment plan and make sound decisions about what they should do that is best for their family.

NMFA believes that surviving spouses need long-term access to counsel and advice concerning the entire benefit package. The surviving family will have questions as the years go by and their benefits and their need for different benefits changes. The young widow with a toddler has too many immediate concerns to think about the child's college education 15 years from now. However, she will be looking one day for information about those benefits. Will she be able to access that information and advice in an easy manner with someone who is an expert in benefits for families? Or, will she be forced to walk into an office where the counselor is more familiar with VA health benefits for veterans than about education benefits for surviving children? The surviving spouse needs information unique to her family, not a cookie cutter, one size fits all answer.

Entities that provide this type of survivor-focused service do exist. For example, Armed Forces Services Corporation (AFSC) has supported the military community for years and is renowned for its expertise in government and military survivor benefits and the survivorship services provided to their military members and families. AFSC's staff provide assistance in matters related to military benefits, Social Security, Veterans' Affairs, and the military SBP, death gratuity, SGLI/Veteran's Group Life Insurance (VGLI), among others. The centerpiece of AFSC's services is their unique software program that provides a personalized projection of the family's integrated stream of government and military survivor benefits, including changes to the benefit amounts throughout the surviving family's lifetime. A service such as this would help surviving families understand and coordinate their benefits in the years to come. Such a service is so valued that presently Army Emergency Relief and the Navy Marine Corps Relief Society present all surviving families of those killed on Active-Duty with lifetime memberships in the Armed Forces Services Corporation to guarantee that they receive the counseling and advice they require.

NMFA recommends the establishment of a survivor office within the VA to provide longterm information and support for surviving spouses and children and offer individualized information about each surviving family's benefit package. A significant element to that support should be access to professional financial counseling.

To a child, the loss of a parent is a life-changing event. As he or she goes through the process of grieving for the parent some help may be required. The VA states that it offers grief counseling to families through its Vet Centers; however, NMFA is concerned about the Department's current capacity to provide that counseling for all who need it. NMFA hopes the VA and DOD will work together to identify the needs of surviving children and promote adequately-resourced programs and initiatives to support those needs.

NMFA recommends that DOD and the VA identify the emotional needs of surviving spouses and children, especially in the area of grief counseling, and promote programs and initiatives to support those needs.

The military service Casualty Assistance Officer (CAO) has received training to help the family through these difficult times. This assistance, however, is performed as an extra duty and the officer is not an expert in survivor issues or financial counseling. Understanding all the benefits and entitlements is a complex process. We have heard from surviving families that they greatly appreciated the help and support provided by the CAO in those first days as he or she served as a representative of their parent service. The presence of the CAO demonstrates to the family that "we take care of our own" and can be a great comfort to the family as they go through the military funeral and honors. Sometimes, however, training for this extra duty can be hurried or incomplete and may result in misinformation or a missed step in a procedure that is not discovered until months down the road with consequences that are irrevocable. Family readiness group leaders and other volunteer support could also benefit from specific training in the area of benefits and support services available for surviving family members.

NMFA recommends improved and consistent training for the CAOs and family support providers so they can better support families in their greatest time of need. Training and responsibilities of CAOs vary by Service. It is only fair to families that they have the best help available.

NMFA has also identified some small fixes to legislation and policy that could help surviving families in their transition process. As we all know, it is often the small inconvenience that may be the straw that breaks the camel's back. Each surviving family has a unique situation. The policy as written now allows the surviving family to remain in government housing for 6 months after the death of the servicemember. This date may come in the middle of a school semester or year. When a child has had to cope with the death of a parent, the consistency and support of their school is important. NMFA recommends that the 6-month limit for occupancy of government quarters or military housing privatized by DOD be waived to allow the children to finish the school year if the family so chooses. Rent would be charged for the extra time.

Guard and Reserve families may choose to keep their employer-sponsored health and dental care when their servicemember is activated and deployed. The family's eligibility for this care may cease if the servicemember is killed on Active-Duty. These families may need information and assistance in making the transition into the TRICARE health system, but they are eligible for the benefit just as if they had been using TRICARE when the servicemember died. However, in the case of the TRICARE Dental Program (TDP), the dental insurance for Active-Duty families, legislative changes are needed to make these families eligible for the benefit available to other survivors. As the law is currently written, only those families enrolled in the TDP at the time of the servicemember's death are eligible to continue enrollment and receive premium free dental insurance for 3 years. NMFA recommends that in cases where the family has employer sponsored dental insurance they be treated as if they had been enrolled in the TDP at the time of the servicemember's death.

NMFA thanks this committee for your attention to the well-being of military families, especially for those who have lost a loved one in service to the Nation. Servicemembers killed on Active-Duty have made the ultimate sacrifice. Their surviving families deserve the most comprehensive package of benefits that a grateful nation can provide. This package should reflect the obligation of the government to compensate the survivors of all servicemembers killed on Active-Duty. It must meet families' short-term needs, provide for their long term financial stability, and recognize the commitment and service of the servicemember and family. With this focus, a grateful Nation can continue to fulfill the promise made to military families by President Lincoln.

APPENDIX 1

Benefits paid by the Department of Defense:

- Death gratuity—$12,420, indexed to increases in basic pay. This is paid to the designated next of kin and is not taxable. This is supposed to be paid within 24 hours of notification of death. The purpose of this payment is to help the survivors in their readjustment and to aid them in meeting immediate expenses.
- Burial benefits—DOD will process, transport, and inter remains. A casket, vault, and headstone are provided or costs of up to $6,900 may be reimbursed if the family elects to make private arrangements. Transportation costs for the immediate family are reimbursed if they must travel for the funeral.
- Military Health and Dental Care Benefits—All otherwise eligible spouses and children remain eligible for military health care coverage. For 3 years from the date of death, TRICARE benefits, including co-pays, remain the same as Active-Duty family benefits. After 3 years, the cost of TRICARE and TRICARE co-pays rise to those of retirees. In most cases, the survivors receive dental insurance premium-free for 3 years, before becoming eligible for the premium-based Retiree Dental Program. The spouse loses eligibility for medical and dental benefits upon remarriage and it may not be reinstated. Children have benefits until age 18 or 23 if enrolled in college.
- Survivor Benefit Plan—Surviving spouses of servicemembers who die on active duty are entitled to SBP benefits. SBP payments equal 55 percent of what the member's retired pay would have been had the member been retired at 100 percent disability, i.e. 75 percent of the basic pay (Basic pay times 75 percent times 55 percent). SBP is automatically adjusted annually for cost of living increases. SBP payments are subject to Federal income taxes. The spouse may decide to waive their payment and have payment made to children only until the children reach age 18 or 23 if enrolled in school. If the spouse remarries before age 55, SBP payments cease. If the subsequent marriage ends in death, divorce or annulment, SBP may be reinstated. If the spouse remarries after age 55, the SBP payments continue. SBP payments are offset by DIC payments.
- Housing benefit—Surviving families may occupy government quarters or be paid housing allowances for 180 days. These allowances vary according to rank and geographic location. In addition, the family is eligible for one move at the cost of the government.

- Servicemember's Group Life Insurance—All servicemembers are automatically enrolled for $250,000 of coverage unless they explicitly decline the insurance or purchase lower levels of coverage. SGLI will be paid to the individual designated on the servicemember SGLI election and certificate form. If no beneficiary is elected by the servicemember, the proceeds are paid first to the surviving spouse; if none, the child(ren) (natural, adopted, or illegitimate) in equal shares; if none, to the parents (natural or adopted).
- Other DOD benefits—Spouses are eligible for Commissary, Exchange, Morale, Welfare, and Recreation activities privileges indefinitely unless they remarry. Children maintain eligibility until age 18 or 23, if still enrolled in college.

Benefits paid by the Department of Veterans' Affairs

- Transition Assistance—a monthly payment of $250 paid to surviving spouses with children for 2 years from the date of death of the servicemember to help with transition.
- Dependency and Indemnity Compensation—Surviving spouses and children (and some dependent parents) are eligible for DIC. The rate has been adjusted annually for cost of living increases. The 2005 spouse DIC rate is $993 monthly. The DIC payment is non-taxable. Additional amounts, also adjusted annually, are authorized for a surviving spouse with minor children. The current monthly benefit is $247 for each child. Unmarried children are eligible for the benefit until they reach the age of 18 (19 if still in secondary school), between 18 and 23 if they are attending a VA approved institution of higher learning or for life if they are disabled while still eligible for the benefit. Children of a deceased member, who did not have a spouse at the time of death, receive a different monthly benefit. If the spouse remarries before age 57, payment of the spouse's DIC ends. The children's DIC payment continues as long as they are eligible. If the subsequent marriage ends in death, divorce or annulment, DIC will be reinstated.
- Survivors' and Dependents' Educational Assistance Program—Surviving spouses and children are eligible for up to 45 months of education benefits. Beginning 1 July 2005, the surviving spouse of a servicemember killed on Active-Duty has an extended eligibility for education benefits of up to 20 years after the date of the member's death. Children are normally eligible to receive the educational benefits between their 18th and 26th birthdays. The current monthly benefit is $803 per month and increases to $824 on 1 October 2005.
- Home Loan Guarantees—An unremarried surviving spouse is eligible for GI home loans and retains eligibility if remarriage occurs after 57th birthday.

Benefits paid by the Social Security Administration:

- Social Security monthly benefits are paid to a spouse or a divorced spouse regardless of age if the children of the deceased servicemember are under age 16 or are disabled and meet social security requirements. The amount paid can only be determined by the Social Security Administration.
- Social Security Lump Sum Death Benefit—a payment of up to $255 is paid to the surviving spouse living with the member at the time of death or to the oldest surviving child if there is no spouse. Some States also pay death benefits or provide other support, especially to the survivors of National Guard or Reserve members killed on Active-Duty. The scope of these benefits and eligibility for them varies by State.

EXAMPLE 1

Servicemember, E-4 over 2 years, age 23, 10th Mountain Division, Fort Drum, NY

Monthly pay and allowances		
Basic Pay	$1,695	
Imminent Danger Pay	225	
Family Separation Allowance	250	
Basic Allowance for Housing	735	
Basic Allowance for Subsistence	267	
Total Pay and Allowances	$3,172	**$38,064 (annual)**
Killed in Line of Duty in Iraq		

Spouse, 22 years old, **2 children** ages 1 and 3
Benefits
Lump Sum payment: Death Gratuity ($12,420), SGLI ($250,000), and Social Security Death Benefit ($255)
Total: $262,675
Education Benefits
Spouse – 45 months at $803 per month – eligible for 20 years
Children – 45 months each at $803 per month – between ages of 18 & 26

Monthly benefits (under current laws, for first six months after servicemember's death)	
DIC for spouse	$ 993
DIC for children $247 each	494
SBP for spouse and children	0*
Social Security (determined by calculator at www.ssa.gov, based on servicemember's income)	1,630
VA Transition Payment	250
BAH (for Fort Drum)	735
Total of monthly benefits	$4,102 ($4802, if choosing "child-only" SBP option)

*SBP spouse annuity payment is $700 per month but is offset by DIC under current law. The family could choose to receive the $700, if the chooses the "Child-only SBP" option.

Changes in Total Annual Benefits (in 2005 dollars)

Years since servicemember's death	Event Triggering Benefit Change	With DIC offset to spouse SBP (current law)	Spouse chooses Child-only SBP	If DIC offset to spouse SBP would be eliminated
immediately	First 6 months (at annual rate), includes Basic Allowance for Housing (BAH)	$49,224	$57,624	$57,624
6 months	End of 1st 6 months (at annual rate): BAH stops	$40,404	$48,804	$48,804
2 years	Beginning of year 3: VA transition payment stops	$37,404	$45,804	$45,804
15 years	Oldest child turns 18, but in college: 30% of Social Security ends	$34,152	$42,552	$42,552
15 years	Youngest child turns 16: Mother's Social Security ends 75%	$26,004	$34,404	$34,404
17 years	Youngest child turns 18 but in college: Social Security ends	$17,844	$26,244	$26,244
19 years	Oldest child turns 23: DIC of $247 ends	$14,880	$23,280	$23,280
21 years Spouse aged 43	Youngest child turns 23: child DIC and SBP for child-only ends	$11,916	$11,916	$20,316

Example 2

Servicemember, E-4 over 2 years, age 23, activated Guard from Topeka, KS

Monthly pay and allowances		
Basic Pay	$1,695	
Imminent Danger Pay	225	
Family Separation Allowance	250	
Basic Allowance for Housing	701	
Basic Allowance for Subsistence	267	
Total Pay and Allowances	$3,172	**$37,656 (annual)**

This does not take into account what the servicemember might have been making at his civilian job and how this affects the family income.
Killed in Line of Duty in Iraq

Spouse, 22 years old, **no children**
Benefits
Lump Sum payment: Death Gratuity ($12,420), and SGLI ($250,000)—Total: $262,420

Education Benefit
Spouse – 45 months at $803 per month – eligible for 20 years

Monthly benefits (under current laws, for first six months after servicemember's death	
DIC for spouse	$ 993
SBP	0*
BAH (for Topeka, KS)	701
Total of monthly benefits	$4,102

*SBP annuity payment is $700 per month but is offset by DIC under current law

Changes in Total Annual Benefits (in 2005 dollars)

Years since servicemember's death	Event Triggering Benefit Change	With DIC offset to spouse SBP (current law)	If DIC offset to spouse SBP would be eliminated
immediately	First 6 months (at annual rate) (With BAH)	$20,328	$28,728
6 months Spouse aged 23	End of 1st 6 months (BAH stops)	$11,916	$20,316

Example 3

Servicemember, E-7 over 14 years, age 34, II Marine Expeditionary Force, Camp Lejuene, NC

Monthly pay and allowances

Basic Pay	$3,249	
Imminent Danger Pay	225	
Family Separation Allowance	250	
Basic Allowance for Housing	974	
Basic Allowance for Subsistence	267	
Total Pay and Allowances	$4,965	**$59,580 (annual)**

Killed in Line of Duty in Iraq

Spouse, 33 years old, **2 children** ages 11 and 13

Benefits

Lump Sum payment: Death Gratuity ($12,420), SGLI ($250,000), and Social Security Death Benefit ($255)—
Total: $262,675

Education Benefits

Spouse – 45 months at $803 per month – eligible for 20 years

Children – 45 months each at $803 per month – between ages of 18 & 26

Monthly benefits (under current laws, for first six months after servicemember's death)

DIC for spouse	$ 993
DIC for children $247 each	494
Spouse SBP	347*
Social Security	3,144
VA Transition Payment	250
BAH (for Camp LeJeune, NC)	974
Total monthly benefits	$6,202

*SBP annuity payment is $1,340 per month but is offset by DIC under current law

Change in Total Annual Benefits (in 2005 dollars)

Years since servicemember's death	Event Triggering Benefit Change	With DIC offset to spouse SBP (current law)	Spouse chooses Child-only SBP	If DIC offset to spouse SBP would be eliminated
immediately	First 6 months (at annual rate) with BAH	$74,424	$86,340	$86,340
6 months	End of 1st 6 months (at annual rate): BAH stops	$62,736	$74652	$74,652
2 years	Beginning of year 3: VA transition pay stops	$59,736	$71,652	$71,652
5 years	Oldest child turns 18 but in college: 30% of Social Security ends	$53,448	$65,364	$65,364
5 years	Youngest child turns 16: Mother's Social Security ends, 75%	$37,728	$49,644	$49,644
7 years	Youngest child turns 18 but in college: Social Security ends	$22,008	$33,924	$33,924
9 years	Oldest child turns 23: DIC for that child ends	$19,044	$30,960	$30,960
11 years Spouse aged 44	Youngest child turns 23: DIC & SBP for child only ends	$16,080	$11,916	$27,996

Example 4

Servicemember, O-5 over 22 years, age 44, 82nd ABN, Fort Bragg, NC

Monthly pay and allowances		
Basic Pay	$6,997	
Imminent Danger Pay	225	
Family Separation Allowance	250	
Jump Pay	150	
Basic Allowance for Housing	1,399	
Basic Allowance for Subsistence	175	
Total Pay and Allowances	$9,196	**$110,352 (annual)**
Killed in Line of Duty in Iraq		

Spouse, 42 years old, **2 children** ages 17 and 18

Benefits

Lump Sum payment: Death Gratuity ($12,420), SGLI ($250,000) and Social Security Death Benefit ($255)—Total: $262,675

Education Benefits

Spouse – 45 months at $803 per month – eligible for 20 years

Children – 45 months each at $803 per month – between ages of 18 & 26

Monthly benefits (under current laws, for first six months after servicemember's death)	
DIC for spouse	$ 993
DIC for child under 18	247
SBP	2,800*
Social Security	1,494
VA Transition Payment	250
BAH (for Fort Bragg)	1,399
Total monthly benefits	$7,183

*SBP annuity payment is $3,793 per month but is offset by DIC under current law

Changes in Total Annual Benefits (in 2005 dollars)

Years after servicemember's death	Event Triggering Change	With DIC offset to spouse SBP (current law)	Spouse chooses Child only SBP	With DIC offset to Spouse SBP eliminated
immediately	First 6 months (at annual rate) with BAH	$86,196	$98,112	$98,112
6 months	End of 1st 6 months (at annual rate): BAH stops	$69,408	$81,324	$81,324
1 year	Youngest child turns 18 but in college: Social Security ends	$51,480	$63,396	$63,396
2 years	Beginning of year 3: VA transition pay ends	$48,480	$60,396	$60,396
5 years Spouse is 47 years old	Youngest child turns 23: DIC & SBP for youngest child ends	$45,516	$11,916	$57,432

The National Military Family Association thanks Senator Jeff Sessions and Senator Joe Lieberman for their active interest in the well being of our military families should the unthinkable happen. NMFA is grateful for the recognition in the HEROES Act of 2005 that the election of insurance is a family decision and for including a provision to ensure that spouses are included in that important decision.

For the family members of a fallen servicemember, NMFA knows that there is no way to compensate them for their loss, only to help them prepare for their future. We strongly believe that all servicemembers' deaths should be treated equally. Servicemembers are on duty 24 hours a day, 7 days a week, 365 days a year. Through their oath, each servicemember's commitment is the same. The survivor benefit package should not create inequities by awarding different benefits to families who lose a servicemember in a hostile zone versus those who lose their loved one in a training mission preparing for service in a hostile zone. To the family, there is no difference. NMFA therefore supports proposals for improvements to the survivor benefit package that are consistent with our philosophy that all Active-Duty deaths be treated equally. We encourage Members of Congress to examine the total package with the goal of recognizing the service and sacrifice of the servicemember and family and providing compensation that promotes the financial stability of the family.

Kathleen B. Moakler, Deputy Director, Government Relations, National Military Family Association, moakler@nmfa.or www.nmfa.org, 703.931.6632, 703.931.4600 (FAX).

Senator LEVIN. Finally, Mr. Chairman, I would ask that the statement of Governor Bill Richardson of New Mexico, who asked to testify here today though it could not be worked out, be placed in the record. He describes in his statement what New Mexico has done for the New Mexico National Guard members who are ordered to Active-Duty. They will pay the premium for the $250,000 SGLI. It is a good example of what States can do to support those who are called to Active-Duty. I would ask that Governor Richardson's statement also be included in the record, as well as a statement from the Gold Star Wives of America. Both of those, Mr. Chairman, would make a real contribution to this record.

Chairman WARNER. Senator Levin, I join you in entering Governor Richardson's statement and these other statements. It has been the intention of the chair to do just that, but I thank you very much.

[The prepared statements of Governor Richardson and the Gold Star Wives of America follow:]

PREPARED STATEMENT BY HON. BILL RICHARDSON

Chairman Warner, Senator Levin, and members of the committee: I appreciate the chance to offer written testimony for today's hearing on death benefits and services available to survivors of military personnel. I would also like to thank Senator Levin for his leadership in the United States Senate, his commitment to our troops at home and those serving abroad and for his efforts to have me testify before the Committee in person today. I believe it's important for today's discussion and future discussions, regarding military death benefits and services available to survivors of military personal, to have the input from our Nation's Governors who serve as the commanders in chief of our respective National Guards.

During this time of war against terrorism, we can all agree that few needs are more pressing, or more deserving of our attention, than taking care of the men and women of the U.S. Armed Forces. However, with longer deployments and meager benefits, the strain on soldiers is unimaginable. The pressures on their families can be unsustainable. The National Guard and Reserves have been called to Active-Duty throughout the world in unprecedented numbers. Few expected to be serving in Iraq or Afghanistan, and fewer still had the time or resources to plan for long deployments.

Meantime, soldiers are still dying. Just last week, 37 of our troops lost their lives in a helicopter crash and in hostile actions while serving in Iraq—the deadliest single day since the war began. While both Democrats and Republicans in Congress have introduced measures to assist those serving abroad as well as their husbands, wives, and children at home, our troops deserve more than speeches. They deserve action.

That is why I have taken it upon myself as Governor of New Mexico to put forth a plan to pay for $250,000 in life insurance for all 4,027 Active-Duty New Mexico National Guard members. New Mexico will become the first State in the country to enact the "Take Care of Our Own" legislation. It comes with an annual cost of $800,000 to the State.

Many Americans may not realize that the current military death benefit pays survivors many already suffering financially during their loved one's deployment—just $12,420. Yesterday, it was reported in an Associated Press article that the administration plans to increase the tax-free "death gratuity," as part of their fiscal year 2006 budget proposal to be submitted to Congress next week. I'm glad to see the administration finally interested in supporting our troops and their families. However, how long will it take before Congress decides to act? I have heard too many stories of families and loved ones left with nothing when their spouse, son or daughter dies in combat. This will never happen again to a family in New Mexico. This is why as the commander in chief of the State National Guard—I chose to act now.

The State Legislature is moving quickly. On Wednesday of last week, the Guard provision passed the New Mexico House 70–0. The New Mexico State Senate may act as early as today. The administration and Congress should follow our lead, doing its part to cover reservists and all military personnel. Washington should act now to provide for the families of our service men and women who fall. There is already national support for such a plan, as we found shortly after launching this initiative. Officials from 20 States, both Republicans and Democrats, have expressed interest in what we're doing. Those states include: Alabama, Arizona, California, Connecticut, Kansas, Kentucky, Maryland, Minnesota, Montana, New Hampshire, New Jersey, New York, Ohio, Oklahoma, Oregon, Pennsylvania, Rhode Island, Tennessee, Texas, and Virginia.

Mr. Chairman, last May, I attended the funeral service for Marine Lance Cpl. Aaron Austin, 21, one of nine New Mexican service personnel killed in Iraq. He died near Fallujah in his second tour. Austin, who had joined the military after the September 11 attacks, left behind a fiancee, family, and friends. At his funeral, I saw proud Americans of humble means suffering an unbearable loss. I vowed then to do something to at least moderate their pain.

This somber story is repeated in communities in every State. A soldier is killed. Those left behind struggle to pay the bills, raise their family, and make ends meet.

As a Governor, I cannot dictate or control benefits for U.S. military personnel, such as the Reserves. But I can help New Mexico National Guard members and their families. I hope we can set a standard for other states, and for our Federal Government, to match National Guard troops and reservists who account for more than 40 percent of our forces in Iraq. That number is expected to grow to 50 percent in the months ahead. About 160,000 Guard troops and reservists are on Active-Duty, including 60,000 in Iraq. Thousands more are being mobilized or are on their way.

When those who serve sacrifice everything, we lose a hero. But their families and loved ones lose much more. When our service men and women are standing vigil on the front lines of the war on terror, they should know that we are behind them and that if they fall, we will take care of their families.

Mr. Chairman and members of the committee, we have a responsibility—a moral duty—to take care of our own—and we will. I look forward to being able to participate in future hearings before the committee, or one of its subcommittees, when it comes to the discussion of death benefits and services available to survivors of military personnel which include our very own National Guard and reservists.

Thank you Mr. Chairman and Senator Levin for hosting this important hearing today.

PREPARED STATEMENT BY THE GOLD STAR WIVES OF AMERICA, INC.

"With malice toward none; with charity for all; with firmness in the right, as God gives us to see right, let us strive to finish the work we are in; to bind up the Nation's wounds. To care for him who has borne the battle his widow and his orphan."

President Abraham Lincoln, Second Inaugural Address, March 4, 1865

The Gold Star Wives of America appreciates the opportunity to participate in this hearing to examine the survivor benefits and the quality of services provided to the family members of those who die in line-of-duty. Please accept our full statement for the record. My name is Edith Smith, and I am the widow of a service connected disabled retired marine.

The new members of Gold Star Wives, represented by our widows here today, have expressed frustration in their letters to you with the present system of Casualty Assistance as well as unanticipated bills they have received for the funerals of their "Fallen Hero." The Casualty Assistance Officer (CAO) does not receive training for this duty, and their prior knowledge of survivor benefits are generally poor. However, our members do express great appreciation for the officers themselves. In order to have some uniform information in the Department of Defense's (DOD) Casualty Assistance program, we would like to acquaint you with the Armed Forces Services Corporation, formerly the benefit department of "Army Air Force Mutual Aid Association" at Fort Myer, Virginia. This group serves as a lifetime casualty assistance office with its unique computer program to project the family's financial future of integrated government survivor benefits from three main sources. They notify their members of all changes to these benefits and assist the surviving spouse in applying for those benefits. Gold Star Wives suggest that Armed Forces Services Corporation be contracted to provide the uniform benefit information to the CAO who will continue to represent the military service and assist the family.

Gold Star Wives thanks the Members of the Senate for seeking ways to improve survivor benefits for family members of this war. We are firm in our belief that "one death, one benefit" should be provided to all surviving spouses of Active-Duty deaths regardless of the cause or place of death. Gold Star Wives is confused to learn that some legislation that would provide more generous survivor benefits to family members who had not been financially dependent on the fallen soldier while denying these same benefits to a financially dependent surviving family of the soldier killed in a "friendly fire" accident in a different location or severely disabled from Iraq.

Gold Star Wives were not included in the legislation last year which improved the survivor benefit payment. My husband paid for me to have the Survivor Benefit Plan (SBP) benefit for 18 years before his death. Were he alive today, our family income would have the disabled retirees offset now eliminated, or if I remarried, my SBP eligibility would be restored. We military widows should not be excluded from the traditional spousal survivor benefit of the DOD.

Gold Star Wives believe the purposes of the SBP and Dependency and Indemnity Compensation (DIC) have been lost. Military widows want the dignity of receiving work-related survivor benefits from our husband's employer. We are appreciative of the DIC paid by the Department of Veterans' Affairs (VA) in recognition of their heroic military service and our great sacrifice.

Gold Star Wives was asked to focus our remarks on the death benefits provided to survivors of the catastrophically disabled retiree. Too many soldiers in this war have horrible permanent injuries caused by improvised explosive devices (IEDs). My own awareness of this often overlooked group rises from my role as the widow of a retired 100 percent disabled marine who died in 1998.

Deaths within 120 days of retirement receive the same benefits and services provided for an Active-Duty death.

The disparities in survivor benefits for the catastrophically disabled arise after 120 days. These families must rise to very difficult challenges that most of us can't begin to imagine. The disparities in death benefits that Gold Star Wives have identified are:

- No death gratuity.
- The VA burial allowance for service-connected deaths of $2,000 plus mileage falls far short of the military's $6,900 allowance. It is sad to know these families will pay to bury their own.
- VA's "special compensation" disabled retirees receive up to $6,709; the surviving spouse receives $993; that is 15 percent of the family income. The surviving spouse of a 100-percent disabled also receives the same indemnity compensation of $993; or 41 percent. My husband lived more than 8 years with a 100-percent disability, so I received an additional $213 DIC for assisting with his care. Soldiers who suffer the most may not live 5 years for their surviving spouse to qualify for this extra $213.
- Casualty Assistance Officers not mandated for retired survivors.
- Life Insurance: the Serviceman's Group Life Insurance (SGLI) must be converted to the Veterans' Group Life Insurance (VGLI) within a short time. The higher cost VGLI is a term insurance with premiums actuarily increased by age, unsubsidized by the government, and with no waiver of premium for permanent disability.
- DIC eligibility is not automatic; cause of death must be service related or live 10 years with the disability. It becomes prudent for the retiree to purchase the military's SBP with a cost of 6½ percent of retired pay to assure his survivor, who has placed her career on hold, of a guaranteed income.
- Surviving family members of retirees are not eligible for 3-year continuation of Active-Duty medical and dental benefits.

Gold Star Wives suggests that the committee restructure survivor benefits for surviving family members of the catastrophically disabled.

WHO WE ARE

Gold Star Wives of America, Inc., is a congressionally-chartered service organization comprised of surviving spouses of military servicemembers who died while on Active-Duty or as a result of a service-connected disability. Many of our membership of over 10,000 are the widows of servicemembers who were killed in combat during World War II, the Korean War, the Vietnam War, and all those military operations up to today's in Iraq and Afghanistan. Almost all of our members are receiving DIC from the VA. Gold Star Wives has been working on Capitol Hill to help maintain survivors benefits since it was founded in 1945. Today, we continue to fight to maintain those benefits for not only our members, but also for the over 330,000 survivors receiving DIC.

Gold Star Wives has a long history of performing volunteer community service as well as volunteer work in our Nation's Veterans Hospitals and many other places where they are needed. During 2003, 119 of our members volunteered in 49 Veterans' Affairs Volunteer Service (VAVS) accredited hospitals and medical centers. Gold Star Wives volunteered at Veterans Hospitals and Medical Centers 11,537 hours valued at $59,416, drove more than 23,866 miles valued at $3,341, and donated over $27,000 in cash and goods. We are currently members of the National VAVS Committee.

The National Legislative Committee of The Gold Star Wives of America is composed of volunteer members. The committee includes:

- Rose Lee, Chairman, of Arlington, Virginia; widow of U.S. Army Active-Duty death; Korean War, Vietnam War;
- Margaret Murphy Peterson of Remsen, New York; widow of a soldier killed in action (KIA); U.S. Army, Vietnam War;
- Penny Splinter of Dubuque, Iowa; widow of KIA, Operation Iraqi Freedom (OIF);
- Edith Smith, of Springfield, Virginia; widow of retired disabled marine, Vietnam War;
- John Brennan, is our paid Washington Government Relations Representative.

SURVIVORS' LEGISLATIVE HIGHLIGHTS IN 108TH CONGRESS

Gold Star Wives worked closely with the Senate Committee on Veterans' Affairs in the 108th Congress to pass legislation that has improved military survivors' benefits. We have always found both majority and the minority committee staff members to work in a bi-partisan and collaborative manner. They have always responded promptly to our requests for information, as well as meetings to discuss our legislative concerns and priorities. Consequently, Gold Star Wives would like to express our gratitude for their efforts in working to improve survivors' benefits during the 108th Congress.

Specific survivors' legislative highlights in the 108th Congress include:

- The Veterans Improvement Act of 2004 (P.L. 108–352)
  - Increases survivors' DIC benefits by $250 per month during the 2-year period following the death of a veteran to further ease the transition of surviving spouses with dependent children;
  - Allows a remarried spouse to be buried in a national cemetery with his or her deceased veteran-spouse and without permission from his or her subsequent husband or wife;
  - Provides for a 10-year extension of delimiting period for Survivors' and Dependents' Educational Assistance (DEA) for spouses of Active-Duty deaths who are now in their first 10-year period of eligibility;
- The Veterans Benefits Act of 2003 (P.L.I08–183)
  - Includes a provision that permits surviving spouses who remarry after attaining age 57 to retain their VA survivors' benefits. Included in that law was a provision that provides for a 1-year period to apply for reinstatement that expired on December 15, 2004, for those who remarried before the law was signed on December 16, 2003. According to the VA, as of last October, 5,794 survivors have applied for reinstatement out of more than 32,000 eligible survivors. Consequently, it does not appear that many were aware of their eligibility to be reinstated. So, we would ask that the law be amended to include those survivors over age 55 as the original legislation requested and to enable those survivors who may not be aware of the legislation to become re-enrolled;
  - Increases the rate of monthly Survivors' and DEA benefits for full time students from $695 to $788 for 45 months (the current full time student rate is $803 per month);
  - Provides for the end of the offset of the SBP payments by DIC payments for survivors who remarry after the age of 57. However, the DOD is refusing to recognize this law and is now seeking to recover payments of the SBP benefits made to survivors who are legally eligible to receive both payments. We would request that the committee help us with this unfair interpretation of the law.

CURRENT SURVIVORS' BENEFITS MONTHLY COMPENSATION

• The VA's Dependency and Indemnity Compensation

DIC is monthly compensation of $993 paid as indemnity to servicemember's surviving spouse. However, this amount is only 41 percent of the $2,429 paid monthly to the family of a veteran who is 100 percent disabled as a result of a service-connected injury. Additionally, the DIC monthly payment of $993 is only 15 percent of the $6,709 monthly payment paid to the catastrophically disabled veteran. Consequently, upon the death of a veteran of a service-connected injury who falls into either disability category, the veteran's family suffers a substantial unanticipated monthly financial setback.

• The DOD's Survivor Benefit Plan

SBP originally was a military retiree's purchased benefit plan that assures a surviving spouse a monthly payment of 55 percent of the monthly retirement check. It was expanded in the 108th Congress to include all line-of-duty deaths without the requirement of 20 years of Active-Duty service after September 10, 2001. However, with the SBP reduced by DIC, practically all Active-Duty deaths result in the survivor receiving only a DIC payment. After November 24, 2003, the OIF survivors have the option to elect the child only SBP. In that case, the SBP benefit is provided to the child without offset of DIC. A sad consequence of the SBP child option is that the survivor who becomes the primary provider for the family, is forced to forego their intended survivor benefit and transfer it for a current income at the unjust loss of a lifetime benefit intended for surviving spouses. No living military retiree is forced to make this option at retirement. We therefore suggest that survivor benefit options provided to the living servicemember should be provided in a similar and equal manner to the deceased member's family. If a divorced spouse is able to obtain SBP benefits for herself as a divorce settlement without offset of any other income, we ask why the survivor cannot be afforded this same benefit as a consequence of their Active-Duty retired spouse's death?

It is extremely hard to understand, from our survivor's perspective, why two wives of one retiree could possibly collect each survivor benefit without offset. Children can collect each benefit without offset, and their years of SBP payments would be longer than the average 7 years a military survivor is expected to live and collect SBP. Another sad result of the child option is that children who are ages 18–23 and in school are paid directly rather than to the surviving parent. Consequently, the survivor has no legal say over this money and it is possible that this dependent child in college could have an income of some $2,000 per month resulting in a loss of potential scholarship and the unusual situation of an unearned income provided directly to the surviving "child."

RECOMMENDATIONS

• Ending the SBP/DIC offset

A servicemember receiving or entitled to receive retirement pay may participate in the SBP to ensure a survivor will have some income in the event of their spouse's death. However, for those retired servicemembers who die as a result of a service-connected disability and therefore entitling their survivor to become eligible for DIC, the survivor's SBP will then be offset dollar for dollar by their DIC.

This patently unfair offset currently affects approximately 52,000 survivors who are dually eligible for both SBP and DIC. While DIC is non-taxable income and SBP is taxable, survivors of these disabled retirees see little or no SBP funds despite having paid monthly premiums equal to 6.5 percent of their retired pay; adding up to thousands of dollars over the years. As a consolation for having made these payments, the accumulated premiums are returned to them without interest. This lump sum refund then becomes a taxable event for the survivor. Unfortunately, there was very little tax advantage for the disabled retiree when paying SBP premiums because his income was predominately non-taxable. Consequently, there is no real advantage to SBP for this group of survivors and, in fact, it becomes an unjust survivor's burden. There is a great deal of resentment by some survivors who see that the Federal Government is collecting taxes on refunded SBP contributions for which they gained nothing financially. The net effect of their monthly premium payments is that the retired disabled veteran's survivor pays taxes for having given the Federal Government a tax free loan.

There is no civilian employer that would be permitted to return many years of survivorship premiums, without interest, should it choose not to pay purchased benefits. Yet, under current law the survivors of a military retiree are denied participation in a cost-sharing benefit that was meant to protect them. Again, had the disabled servicemember retired from Federal civil service, the survivor would be entitled to both the civil service survivor benefit and DIC, with no offset.

Many SBP/DIC survivors have spent more than 20 years sacrificing and supporting their spouse's military career and then years taking care of them during their years of disability. Retired pay represents deferred compensation for the 20 or more years of military service and disability pay that is designed to compensate for a veteran's reduction in quality of life and lost future earnings as a result of his sacrifice for his country. Just as the disabled military retirees are now entitled to both benefits, so should their survivors. Many survivors are in their 50s or older and have not had the opportunity to develop their own careers. The DIC attempts to indemnify them for the loss of a spouse's life and an element of support for their future. The SBP represents completely different income that they have paid for and made a life of sacrifices for like multiple deployments, constant anxiety about their spouse's well being, frequent moves, and no real chance to invest in a pension of their own.

- Better training for the Casualty Assistance Officers

We raise this issue as we have heard of many instances of problems that the new survivors of the conflicts in Iraq and Afghanistan have experienced. For most survivors, the death of their spouse is the most catastrophic event of their lives. Many are literally in shock for many months and are unable to cope with the financial decisions and bureaucratic tangles that a survivor encounters. The CAOs are unfortunately not now adequately trained, nor are any assigned to such duty full time. Yet, they must try to help survivors go through the maze of the VA and DOD benefits. CAOs cannot provide the kind of counseling, both grief counseling and financial counseling necessary to meet the needs of a military survivor. There currently is little guidance for the CAOs. Without training or some DOD/VA/Social Security (SS) integrated brochures, survivors are without proper counseling and guidance at a critical time in their lives. All of the services should have standardized guides.

A suggested solution to provide uniform and accurate information to all survivors would be for DOD to contract with the Armed Forces Services Corporation (AFSC). AFSC specializes in government survivor benefits and is renowned for its expertise, outstanding service, and its unique computer program that projects the family's future integrated stream of government survivor benefits and changes that occur to those amounts due to changing ages of the spouse and children. They serve as a lifetime casualty assistance office keeping their members informed of legislative changes that may affect the family's survivor benefits and assist the surviving spouse in applying for those benefits. AFSC assists the surviving spouse in dealing with the DOD, VA, and the Social Security Administration (SSA).

- Improved upfront information needed for survivors' decisions

Survivors need to know upfront the following information:

-Upon remarriage survivors are subject to the following change in benefits:

-Loss of their military ID card and consequent loss of base privileges including Exchange and Commissary, morale, welfare, and recreation (MWR), and military medical benefits;

-Their medical benefits can go from TRICARE to CHAMPVA.

-Military survivors who work for the Federal Government can be barred from receiving their spouse's Social Security benefit;

-Those not enrolled in Medicare Part B are not eligible for CHAMPVA. The waiver of penalties and interest assessed for late enrollment has been fixed legislatively for TRICARE but not for CHAMPVA. Gold Star Wives would like to respectfully suggest that the plain language of Title 38, Section 1713 gives these CHAMPVA widows the same or similar benefits as TRICARE survivors. We are told that about 60–100 disabled widows may be suffering a loss of medical care because they were unaware of the mandated requirement to purchase Medicare Part B as an additional condition to their eligibility for CHAMPVA. We ask the committee to inquire as to the welfare of these widows.

- The creation of a Survivors' Office within the VA and/or the DOD

There currently is no central focus or location within either the VA or DOD that a survivor or family member can go to with questions or concerns about their benefits. The VA's regional offices are woefully inadequate at providing information concerning survivors' benefits. DOD likewise has no central location for the new survivor to turn to should their CAO be without such information. There is virtually no coordination between DOD and VA that survivors can count on. Consequently, there is a need for a Survivors' Office that can carry out these critical functions from a central location.

- Future changes in survivors' benefits

There are several bills being introduced concerning proposed changes to survivors' benefits, including an increase in the death gratuity from $12,000 to $100,000 and an increase in life insurance. We strongly recommend that any changes made to survivors' benefits should not differentiate between Active-Duty deaths and KIA deaths. Survivors of servicemembers who die on Active-Duty have very similar experiences and needs following their loss. Also, insurance proceeds should go to the servicemember's surviving spouse and any children, rather to other family members who may not be dependents.

BIOGRAPHY OF EDITH SMITH

Edith Smith is the widow of a disabled military retiree, Lt. Col. Vincent M. Smith, USMC, Ret. He had the misfortune to suffer a disabling heart condition in 1987, at age 48. Twenty-nine months later, Vince was switched to Medicare and his earned military health benefit of retirement, CHAMPUS was unexpectedly terminated simply because his disabling condition met the strict requirements for a swift and unchallenged Social Security disability determination. With the special help of Senator John McCain, Arizona, and Congressman Bill Young, Florida, Edith set out in 1991 to change the law with another wife (residing in Florida) whose husband suffered a traumatic brain injury at about age 50. Within 10 months, legislation restoring CHAMPUS as second payer to Medicare was signed into law for about 100,000 retired Medicare eligibles under age 65. A July 19, 1992, segment describing the mission of Terry Cox and Edith to change the law ran on Tom Brokaw's NBC "Nightly News." Mr. Brokaw ended the segment with his comment: "Hell hath no fury like a woman scorned with a phone and a fax!"

Edith has continued her role as a volunteer advocate for Disabled Military Beneficiaries by serving as a member of the TRICARE Beneficiary Working Task Force at Tricare Management Activity in Falls Church, Virginia. In her volunteer capacity, she has prepared and presented testimony more than 20 times since 1993 before various congressional committees as a citizen advocate working to correct unjust problems that surfaced with the implementation and integration of the dual Medicare/CHAMPUS/TRICARE benefit for those under age 65. Following her husband's death, Edith focused her efforts on changes to the "custodial care" definition in order to provide medically necessary care to children requiring skilled nursing delivered in the home setting.

Edith continues to serve in a volunteer role as a resource on disabled issues to the Government Relations Department of The National Military Family Association and to The National Association for Uniformed Services. In 1998, The National Military Family Association honored Edith with their prestigious Margaret Vinson Hallgren Award for her efforts on behalf of the disabled members of the military community. She served in various positions on The Advisory Social Services Board to Fairfax County Board of Supervisors for 7 years. She became a member of Gold Star Wives of America shortly after her husband's death and assists with their Washington legislative activities.

A native Virginian, Edith graduated from Mary Washington College of the University of Virginia in 1962 with a Bachelor of Science degree in Home Economics Education. She was married to Vince Smith for 35 years, staying at home to assist with his care during the years of his disability. They have two children; Karen, her husband Chas, one son Steve and two grandchildren.

DISCLOSURE STATEMENT

Neither Edith Smith nor the Gold Star Wives of America, Inc. have received any Federal Grant or contract during the current or previous 2 fiscal years relative to the subject matter of this testimony.

Chairman WARNER. Senator Levin, this marks our 27th year that you and I have been together on this committee. Through those years, I can say without any equivocation whatsoever, you have been at the very forefront of all these personnel issues, and you speak from the heart.

Senator LEVIN. You are our leader, Mr. Chairman, and we are grateful for that.

Chairman WARNER. I think there have been times when you have been the leader of this committee. It seems to me it goes back and forth.

Senator LEVIN. I am not going there, Mr. Chairman. [Laughter.]

Chairman WARNER. The chair also notes that Senator Frist, the Majority Leader, has put in legislation, as well as Senator Craig and Senator Akaka. On the Veterans Committee, you will be having a hearing very shortly on this matter, will you not, Senator Akaka?

Senator AKAKA. Mr. Chairman, thank you very much for recognizing me.

I want to pay tribute, Mr. Chairman, to our military members and their families serving our country presently.

I want to take this opportunity to welcome our panel here and to thank you for your leadership to our country. Thank you for coming today to provide us with information that we consider very serious to our Nation with respect to benefits and services available to the survivors of our military personnel.

I want to say that this is very important to me, because I serve as the ranking member of the Senate Veterans' Affairs Committee with my friend and leader and chairman, Larry Craig from Idaho. I want you to know that we will also be holding a hearing on this issue on Thursday, and we certainly look forward to that.

Thank you very much, Mr. Chairman.

Chairman WARNER. Thank you, Senator Akaka. The chair also notes that you proudly served our Nation in World War II as a member of the United States Army. We are proud to have you on this committee.

Senators Kennedy and Clinton on this committee likewise, Senator Levin, have been very active in this legislation, as I had mentioned with Senator Frist, the Majority Leader, and we also have Senator DeWine. You took a lead on legislation. The committee would like to invite you to address the committee at this time.

STATEMENT OF HON. MIKE DEWINE, U.S. SENATOR FROM THE STATE OF OHIO

Senator DEWINE. Mr. Chairman, thank you very much. Let me thank you and Senator Levin for this hearing. Let me also congratulate Senators Sessions, Lieberman, Allen, and Nelson for your work.

I have had the experience I think, Mr. Chairman, that many of us have had, the very sad experience, of meeting with and seeing children of servicemen who have been killed in Iraq and Afghanistan, some of them only 2, 4, and 6 years old. We have also seen or read about situations where our young men have left children they have never seen. We had that situation in Ohio just this past week.

I think, Mr. Chairman, this causes us to wonder what will become of these children financially. We know how sad it is to lose a parent. We think about that. I think there is an obligation that we all feel as a country to make sure that that child is taken care of. So I would ask this committee, as you begin to work on formulating legislation, to think about that.

The proposal that the Pentagon has put forward is good. I welcome that. I congratulate the administration for that. But quite frankly, I think it is lacking in a couple areas.

The current monthly payment for the child is $247. I think that, if we look at the situation today with families, it is inadequate. The bill that I have introduced would raise that to $750. There is nothing magical about $750, but I think it is a much more reasonable amount of money, and I would ask the committee to take a look at that.

The second thing is education. You wonder about the education for these children. Giving a death benefit and increasing the death benefit today is interesting. That is good. I think we should do that. But some of these children are 1 and 2 years old. 16 or 17 years from now, I worry about the education for the child.

What the bill that Senator Durbin and I have introduced would do is to raise the amount of money available per child from $36,000 to $80,000. That is commensurate, frankly, with about what it costs to go to a State university. Our bill also would allow that money to be spent not only for tuition, but also for room and board. That is a rational thing to do. It is commensurate and consistent with what a parent would do if you were providing for your child or trying to help your child. You would not distinguish between room and board and tuition. You would allow the money to be used for whatever it took that child to go to college.

I think, Mr. Chairman, that is the least we can do for the children of the service men and women who have given their lives for our country.

I thank the chair.

Chairman WARNER. Thank you very much, Senator.

We have a quorum present and we have to comply with the rules of the Senate. So I am going to ask your indulgence. Senator Levin and I submit this jointly to our committee.

I ask the committee to consider a resolution for committee funding for the 109th Congress and to adopt committee rules for this Congress. Under the Senate rules, each committee is required to report out a resolution at the beginning of each Congress authorizing the committee to make expenditures of the contingent fund of the Senate to defray its expenses, including staff salaries and administrative expenses, for a 2-year period.

The committee staff, majority and minority, has worked together to prepare this resolution on the committee budget. Senator Levin and I reviewed the budget and jointly recommend it to the committee. The proposed budget is in line with the funding guidelines provided by the Rules Committee and consistent with the joint leadership agreement of January 6th, 2005. The budget represents a freeze at the committee's funding level for the 108th Congress, increased only by cost-of-living adjustments (COLAs).

Is there a motion to have this resolution reported out favorably?

Senator LEVIN. So moved.

Chairman WARNER. Is there a second?

Senator LIEBERMAN. Second.

Chairman WARNER. The motion is agreed to. All in favor, say aye. [A chorus of ayes.]

Opposed? [No response.]

The ayes have it.

In addition, the committee must adopt its rules for the 109th Congress. Senator Levin and I reviewed the rules and recommend only minor technical changes. The corrections are before you.

Is there a motion to adopt the rules?

Senator LEVIN. So moved.
Chairman WARNER. Is there a second?
Senator LIEBERMAN. Second.
Chairman WARNER. Hearing a second, all in favor, say aye. [A chorus of ayes.]
Opposed? [No response.]
The ayes have it.
I thank the members, and this will appear in the record.
The record should also reflect that Senator Hagel has been very active in this legislation likewise. He is a veteran of the Vietnam conflict, a decorated veteran.
I think at this point in time, unless other members indicate to the chair a need to speak, I would like to recognize the witnesses. Dr. Chu, would you proceed.

STATEMENT OF HON. DAVID S.C. CHU, UNDER SECRETARY OF DEFENSE FOR PERSONNEL AND READINESS

Dr. CHU. Good morning, Mr. Chairman, Senator Levin. I want to thank you both, and I thank members of the committee for the opportunity to appear this morning and to offer an overview of how we treat those who are severely wounded in the current conflict and the benefits available to those who give their lives for our country.
Chairman WARNER. Dr. Chu, I would like to also recognize your long service to our Nation in your capacity in the DOD. I understand that you may be rejoining your family from this long absence in the near future. So we thank you.
Dr. CHU. Thank you very much, Senator. I appreciate it.
I want to thank you also, both you and Senator Levin, for recognizing the contribution that the coalition forces have made in the Middle East, with the opportunity they have given Iraq for a first election in decades that was free and open and gives the people of that country a real set of choices.
I am honored to be joined this morning by the Vice Chiefs of the military departments and Mr. Epley from the Veterans' Affairs Department.
I do have a statement for the record which I hope I can submit.
Chairman WARNER. Without objection, the statement of Dr. Chu and other witnesses will be admitted to the record in full.
Dr. CHU. Thank you, Mr. Chairman.
I also want to join in the sentiment that the members of the committee have expressed, and the Department believes is fundamental in how we view the issues before us this morning, and that is, there is nothing in the financial sense that we can do to replace a lost servicemember. We recognize that.
We recognize also for those severely wounded we cannot necessarily, with financial means, compensate that individual for the grievous wound that he or she has suffered. But we can make their lives comfortable. We can give them the appropriate financial tools with which to move forward, and that really is the focus of my comments this morning.
As this committee is aware, we have transformed medical care in this set of conflicts since September 11, 2001. We do things very differently from the way we did before, starting with how we pro-

tect our people, the widespread use of lightweight body armor, the change in how we care for the wounded, bringing them promptly back to an area, usually the United States, where they can receive definitive care. We think this has reduced the rate of death. We think it has also allowed us to care more appropriately for the wounds that are received, although I acknowledge the armor has changed the nature of the wounds that are endured in this conflict. We are proud of the fact that we have the lowest death and non-battle injury rate in the recorded history of our country in any major conflict in this ongoing set of operations.

We have, we believe, a good set of programs to take care of those who are severely wounded. Each Service is moving to build a case management capability, the marines expanding their Marine for Life program, the Army with its Disabled Soldier Support System (DS3). We are creating a joint operations center to ensure that no one falls through the cracks, and that the ability of the families to put together the various programs available to them, if a servicemember is grievously wounded, is properly sustained. That center will actually be formally inaugurated today. If any members of the committee wish to be present, I certainly would be delighted to invite you to join us.

We will have a 1–888 number for the family members to call if they feel they have questions that they have not yet been able to ask. That number is 1–888–774–1361.

Let me turn, if I may, very briefly to the issue of death benefits, which is the focus, I think, of most of the discussion in your comments this morning. Congress, as Senator Sessions has noted, has asked us to work with them over the last 2 years, starting with the National Defense Authorization Act of Fiscal Year 2004 which commissioned two studies, one by the Government Accountability Office (GAO), and one independent study the DOD was asked to inaugurate and that we invited the SAG Corporation to complete. Those studies have been submitted to you.

In your National Defense Authorization Act for Fiscal Year 2005, you requested that we should report, with the President's budget, summarizing our conclusions from those studies and our own work on this important subject. We are prepared to do so. I would like to very briefly this morning summarize our major findings.

First of all, as a number of members have noted, the United States Government already provides a significant set of programs to help the families of those who give their lives in service to the country. We calculate that in the typical case of a surviving spouse and young children, the income replacement programs approximately substitute, dollar for dollar, what the military member was earning on active service, and by military compensation we mean what we call regular military compensation. That is the sum of basic pay, quarters, and subsistence allowances, and the tax advantages thereon. So we have a good program, we would argue, of income support for a family with young children which loses the servicemember.

The family is also eligible, as has been noted this morning, for a variety of other benefits. We provide transitional housing assistance. The family can stay in the Government housing and receive an allowance for 6 months. We provide access, on a lifetime basis really, for the surviving spouse to the TRICARE system and for the children until they reach adulthood. We also provide lifetime access to the spouse to the commissary and exchange system. We do provide, as Senator DeWine has noted already, through the VA, an important educational benefit both for the spouse and for the surviving children.

Where we conclude we need to strengthen what we are doing—and that is the focus of the bill that Senator Sessions has introduced, is what you might call a bequest, the single cash payment that comes to the family upon the servicemember's death. That currently is just over $260,000: That is to say, the sum of the SGLI payment of $250,000 and what people call the death gratuity, currently set at $12,420. We believe that sum ought to be nearer to $500,000, and we propose to change that by increasing the amount covered by the SGLI policy, as well as increasing what people like to call the death gratuity.

I might say, as an aside, that I hope we can work with the committee to find a different term for what is now called the death gratuity. That really, I think, is a bit of an anachronism in terms of terminology. It is not really indicative, as I listened to the comments this morning and elsewhere, of what the country wants to do. The country wants to recognize the service of these individuals and express its condolences for the loss of the servicemember.

We look forward to working with the members of this committee, as we have already done, as Senator Sessions indicated, over the last year-plus or so, in terms of providing to our service people and their surviving families what they deserve in the difficult circumstances they face today.

Thank you, Mr. Chairman.

[The prepared statement of Dr. Chu follows:]

PREPARED STATEMENT BY HON. DAVID S.C. CHU

INTRODUCTION

Mr. Chairman and members of this distinguished committee, thank you for the opportunity to be here today. It is my privilege to discuss the means by which we care for the severely wounded, as well as the surviving families of deceased military personnel.

Support to the Severely Wounded:

Each of the Services has initiated an effort to ensure that our seriously wounded servicemembers are not forgotten—medically, administratively, or in any other way. To facilitate a coordinated response, the Department of Defense (DOD) has established a Joint Support Operations Center (JSOC). We are collaborating, not only with the military Services, but also with other departments of the Federal Government, nonprofit organizations, and corporate America, to assist these deserving men and women and their families.

A number of our severely injured servicemembers will be able to return to duty, thanks to their dedication and commitment, and the phenomenal quality of military medicine. Some, however, will transition from the military and return to their hometowns or become new members of another civilian community. These are capable, competent, goal-oriented men and women—the best of our Nation. We will ensure that during their rehabilitation we provide a "case management" approach to advocating for the servicemember and his or her family. From the Joint Support Operations Center here, near the seat of government, to their communities across America, we will be with them. This will continue through their transition to the Department of Veterans' Affairs (VA), and the many other agencies and organizations providing support to them.

I have mentioned that the JSOC is a collaborative effort, both inside and outside the government. I recognize and appreciate the interest and express desire of Congress to help ensure the success of this effort. As we identify the need for statutory changes, we will be certain to make you aware and seek your assistance.

Twenty-four hours a day, 7 days a week, 365 days a year, we are a toll-free phone call away. We will provide a venue for each of the separate programs to be successful, while ensuring that no one falls through a crack. The center will be a one-stop location, providing a central point of contact for information and support.

PREVENTING INJURIES

The DOD actively pursues all methods to prevent our military members from bodily harm. As technology has dramatically advanced from previous wars, the military has increased its lethality, but our equipment is safer, and our warfighter is more highly skilled.

With your support, we strive to provide the best military equipment in the world and ensure that it is safe to operate. For example, we believe that body armor, helmets, and protective vests, are reducing both hostile and accidental serious injuries. This is supported by preliminary analysis, which indicates that most injuries are to the body extremities, arms and legs, with less severe injuries to the head and torso areas.

Secretary Rumsfeld's initiative to change how the DOD views the safety of its military personnel and civilian employees also has made an impact. Our goal is zero preventable mishaps. We have taken a major step in that direction. We are succeeding in Operation Iraqi Freedom (OIF). Historically, about half of the Army's wartime losses were due to accidents; in OIF, about 26 percent of the losses result from preventable mishaps.

When injuries do occur, far-forward medical and surgical resuscitation, en route critical care support, and rapid evacuation to definitive care have significantly reduced combat-related deaths. This is very evident in OIF as we have a ratio of only one battle death for every ten wounded in action, compared to ratios for previous wars that ran typically around 1 to 3. With improved treatment we are also seeing 48 percent of the wounded in Iraq return to their units within 72 hours.

Similarly, our military health system has made significant advances in the prevention of injury and disease. These include public health measures, immunization of servicemembers, use of early detection techniques against biochemical agents, and pre- and post-deployment assessments. These have been particularly beneficial in prevention and early detection and treatment of disease and non-battle injuries. Consequently, disease/non-battle injury rates have been lower than in any other conflict.

DEATH BENEFITS

We realize first that no benefits can replace a human life. The lost presence of the family member is what the survivors face. We can't provide that, nevertheless, we must try to address the difficult issue of how to compensate these survivors. Permit me to offer you an overview of what we do in response to the loss of a military member, including personal assistance, as well as cash benefits.

Our system of benefits is generally good, but our recent assessment, in response to your direction, concluded that the overall package could be improved to honor properly the contributions and sacrifices of our servicemembers. We are working within the DOD and with other agencies to address these deficiencies, primarily in the area of immediate cash compensation, for those whose death is the result of hostile actions. We are looking at ways to improve the lump sum payments through increased insurance and death gratuity payments. I will address these in more detail later.

MILITARY CASUALTY ASSISTANCE

When a military member dies, our first concern is to inform the next-of-kin in a manner that is fast, efficient, and highly respectful. Our military casualty assistance program is highly developed and well suited to perform this difficult task effectively. Notification is made in person by Casualty Assistance Officers (CAOs) who are customarily accompanied by a chaplain.

CAOs personnel stay with the family following notification of the loss, through funeral preparations, burial, and the entire process of determining benefits and compensation. They provide valuable counsel and support to the families, arranging for the military funeral (if desired), running interference when problems arise, and ensuring that the families receive the benefits and compensation due them. The families know that they can contact their Casualty Assistance Office representative at any time, even long after the servicemember's death. We are proud of our Casualty

Assistance program. We often hear from the families that they consider their Casualty Assistance Office representative "part of the family."

The DOD continuously explores how it can better support our family members during the most tragic of times, the loss of a loved one in the service to our Nation.

One such initiative is the expedited claims process (ECP) with the Social Security Administration (SSA). In March 2003, we partnered with the SSA to study the possibility of institutionalizing the ECP that was so effective in the tragic aftermath of September 11, 2001. The ECP incorporates post-adjudicative development of evidence, as well as the use of a special toll free number for applicants and CAOs to call when they are ready to file. This process has been extremely successful in providing swift financial assistance to our families. The final results of the pilot program showed the average claims processing time dropped from several weeks to an average of just over 2 days time. Accordingly, the ECP was made permanent in January 2004 for surviving family members of all Active-Duty casualties. We established a similar arrangement with the VA several years ago. That program has also significantly expedited the delivery of compensation and benefits to our families.

BENEFITS FOR SURVIVORS

Benefits for survivors vary significantly in purpose and method of payment. Some are immediate cash payments or reimbursements for costs incurred; others provide long-term monthly income. These benefits are typically available whether the death is a result of hostilities, the result of non-hostile duty-related activities, or even the result of disease or off-duty injuries.

Death Gratuity Benefit

The first benefit is to provide an infusion of cash to alleviate immediate financial requirements. This is accomplished by the death gratuity payment (currently $12,420, indexed to inflation). Our intent is to provide this payment in conjunction with the notification of death or as quickly thereafter as possible. This is done at the local level and normally takes place within 24 hours.

Funeral Costs

One of the first expenses survivors encounter is for the funeral. DOD will reimburse some or all such expenses the family pays directly. The amount payable varies depending which government services are provided. If the family pays all costs, it qualifies for up to $6,900 in reimbursements for these services.

Insurance Proceeds

After the funeral, the most substantial benefit is the life insurance proceeds from personal policies as well as from Servicemembers' Group Life Insurance (SGLI). This is our principal insurance program and is under the purview of the VA, operated by the Office of Servicemembers Group Life Insurance (OSGLI), an arm of Prudential. SGLI provides up to $250,000 of coverage for modest premiums paid by the member. The DOD pays any costs associated with an increased number of deaths attributable to the extra hazards of military service compared to the number of deaths expected in peacetime.

Housing-in-kind or Cash Allowance

A surviving family may continue to live in military housing without cost for up to 6 months after the member's death. This enables the member's family to reorient their lives without undue pressure to relocate immediately. They are able to make choices about the future in an orderly manner. Should the family not occupy military housing or move out of military quarters before the end of those 6 months, they receive a cash allowance in lieu of quarters. In essence, we provide 6 months of transitional rent.

Medical Benefits

Surviving family members continue to qualify for military medical benefits. For the first 3 years, health benefits remain at the same level of care as if the member were still on Active-Duty. Family members are then provided medical coverage at the same level as for the families of retired members. Children remain qualified until age 23, and spouses so long as they do not remarry.

Continued Military Community Privileges

Surviving family members continue to be eligible for use of the Commissary and Exchange, and military morale, welfare, and recreation facilities. These privileges continue under the same qualifying criteria that otherwise apply if the member were retired.

Monthly Cash Compensation

The surviving family typically qualifies for one or more monthly cash benefits under plans administered by the DOD, the VA, and the SSA. Taken together, the surviving spouse with minor children will typically qualify for monthly benefits that are equal to or even exceed the former income of the member. These payments are reduced in the event of remarriage before a certain age. Although Survivor Benefit Plan (SBP) payments from DOD are taxable as income, little or any tax will apply if the payments are made to the children. The VA Dependency and Indemnity Compensation (DIC) benefit is not taxable. Social Security payments can be taxable depending on the other income, but would probably be minimal for a survivor with little or no other income. Thus, the income provided the surviving family would carry little or no tax liability.

VA Monthly DIC

DIC is provided by the VA to the surviving spouse with additional payments for children. For a spouse and two children, this benefit is $993 monthly plus $247 per child (plus if there are children under age 18, $250/month for 2 years). This equates to $20,844 of tax-free income annually for the first 2 years, and $17,844 thereafter so long as the children are not of age (the benefit for a spouse alone is $11,916 annually for life or until remarriage if before age 57). The DIC is fixed for all veterans regardless of rank in service.

DOD Survivor Benefit Plan

The family also qualifies for a monthly payment from DOD equal to 55 percent of the retired pay the member would have received if he or she had retired for total disability on the date of death. This retired pay is computed as 75 percent of the member's average basic pay over the last 3 years. If the spouse alone qualifies for this benefit, the DIC is subtracted from the SBP. However, it may be paid instead to the children and the benefits are then additive for as long as the youngest child qualifies (about age 22).

Social Security Survivor Benefit

Military members participate in social security on their basic pay and thus qualify for the same benefits as any other covered worker. This means monthly payments for children as well as to the surviving spouse with young children (up to age 16). These benefits depend on the history of covered wages under the Social Security program.

The table below summarizes these income benefits for married O–3s and E–6s with two children as well as a married E–6 with no children, and a single E–6. For a married E–6 with two children (8 years of service), the total of these three programs pays more than 110 percent of the member's final rate of Regular Military Compensation (RMC). For a married O–3 with children, the total equates to 96 percent of RMC. In both cases, much of the income is tax free. Thus, the family's after tax income could actually be higher than RMC.

Education Benefits from the VA

Education benefits from the VA are quite valuable and are available to both the spouse and the children. These benefits are payable for up to 45 months of education time and can easily exceed $100,000 for a spouse and two children.

Estimated Death Benefits

Benefit	Amount	O-3 Married with 2 Children	E-6 Married with 2 Children	E-6 Married No Children	E-6 Single	Remarks
RMC at Time of Death	Salary Equivalent	$77,350	$51,877	$52,238	$49,574	
DoD Payments						
Death Gratuity	$12,420	$12,420	$12,420	$12,420	$12,420	One-Time Payment
Burial Expense	$6,900	$6,900	$6,900	$6,900	$6,900	Reimbursed Maximum
Housing Cost and Relocation	Housing or Allowance	$8,378	$7,316	$7,316	$0	Equal to 6 months BAH
Survivor Benefit Plan (SBP)	55% of Total Disability Retired Pay	$20,166	$11,028	$0	$0	Annual to Children or Spouse net of DIC
VA Administered Benefits						
SGLI	$250,000	$250,000	$250,000	$250,000	$250,000	Full Coverage
VA DIC	$993 monthly plus $247/Chld (Plus $250/month for 2 years)	$20,844	$20,844	$11,916	$0	Spouse with Added Amounts for Children
VA Education*	$803/mo for Spouse & Children	$108,405	$108,405	$36,135	$0	Up to 45 Months Each
Benefits Administered by Social Security Administration						
Social Security Benefits	Based on rules of SSA	$33,547	$25,067	$0	$0	SSA Calculator
Total Payments						
Total Amounts	Up Front	$277,698	$276,636	$276,636	$269,320	
Total Amounts	Annual	$74,557	$56,939	$11,916	$0	
Benefits from DoD*						
Unused Leave	Varies	$4,586	$2,604	$2,604	$2,604	Assume 30 Days
Health Care First 3 Years	TRICARE health coverage	$15,000 / Yr	$15,000 / Yr	$15,000 / Yr	$0	Based on FEHBP
Health Care After First 3 Years	TRICARE health coverage	$12,000 / Yr	$12,000 / Yr	$12,000 / Yr	$0	Plan with Deductibles
Commissary and Exchange	Actual Savings Based on Expenses	$2,500 / Yr	$2,500 / Yr	$2,500 / Yr	$0	Standard for 3 Persons

* Not included in Totals Above, value depends on use, the max is equal to $803 x45 mos. = $36,135 for spouse alone and $36,135 x 3 = $108, 405 for spouse and 2 children

Taxable Payments
Member has 8 Years of Service

Financial Counseling

A final, but important benefit is the financial counseling available to survivors. There are many associations that provide such benefits, some of them chartered for special status by Congress, for example, the Mutual Aid Associations. Each has programs that help members and survivors understand their benefits. Anyone who receives proceeds under the SGLI program qualifies to receive continuing financial counseling service through a program set up by the VA. The Beneficiary Financial Counseling Service (BFCS) provides a highly valuable benefit for survivors. This program provides a comprehensive assessment of the lifetime financial plan of beneficiaries, including a full presentation of the benefits described in this paper.

We are currently in the process of testing a Servicemembers Benefit Analysis program through an Army pilot. We are also developing simple spreadsheet tools to help describe available benefits for service personnel. We expect to see rapid improvement in our capability to deliver financial counseling over the next several months.

ADEQUACY OF BENEFITS

The National Defense Authorization Act for Fiscal Year 2004 included a requirement for us to study the totality of all current and projected death benefits for survivors of deceased members of the Armed Forces. The study was to include a comparison of military with other Federal death benefits as well as with commercial and other private sector death benefit plans. The GAO was to conduct a similar study.

To ensure an independent review, we contracted for the study with the SAG Corporation. SAG completed the study in June 2004. The study concluded that the system of benefits provided to survivors of members who die on Active-Duty to be adequate, substantial and comprehensive. However, it identified areas where improvements could make the benefits more comparable to benefits provided by other employers. For example, many large employers provide some insurance at no cost. The rationale of providing Federal benefits in recognition of deaths in the performance of duty of law-enforcement officers and firefighters, would seem to apply as well to military members.

GAO's report, dated July 2004, "Survivor Benefits for Servicemembers and Federal, State, and City Government Employees" made no recommendations, but reached findings similar to the SAG report. GAO found servicemembers almost always obtain higher lump sums than do the survivors of 61 civilian government entities, but the survivors of civilian government employees in some high-risk occupations may receive supplemental benefits. These supplemental payments generally result in higher benefits to employees in these high-risk occupations than for servicemembers.

As you can see from the foregoing, the benefits provided are substantial. They come from a wide variety of programs and address a variety of concerns. They provide significant continuing income and are of great help to survivors in making their transition through the changes in life that inevitably follow a member's death. A surviving spouse with young children has the potential to receive more than $2 million over her or his remaining lifetime.

We agree with the findings of the SAG and GAO reports that our benefits, while substantial, do not provide specific recognition of deaths that occur when our members are sent into harms' way in the service of their Nation; so we propose increasing the cash benefits for deaths that occur under these circumstances. We support the principle that the surviving family of a member killed in combat should receive about $500,000. This compares to the approximately $262,000 they are able to receive today. We advocate doing this by: (1) Increasing the maximum SGLI to $400,000 with $150,000 of insurance funded by the Government when the member is serving in an operation or area designated by the Secretary of Defense; (2) Increasing the current $12,420 death gratuity to $100,000 for deaths occurring in these same designated areas; and (3) Applying these improvements retroactively to the beginning of Operation Enduring Freedom (OEF) and OIF. We intend to fund these enhancements within planned appropriations or budgeted levels.

These improvements I have outlined in benefits are an outgrowth of the conclusions in both the SAG and the GAO reports that I discussed above. We have drafted language to make these improvement and are eager to move this legislation forward. Our bill, while not identical, is broadly consistent with other bills already introduced in the 109th Congress, such as the HEROES Act of 2005.

Our objective is to ensure that we fully support our servicemembers when we send them in harm's way, and that we properly support the family's needs if the servicemember dies on Active-Duty.

Chairman WARNER. Thank you very much, Dr. Chu. I think that is an important aside you had. We will study that issue and I share the thoughts and will work with you.

My understanding is that Deputy Secretary of Defense Wolfowitz worked actively with you, Senator Sessions, as this legislation was drawn up. Am I correct in that?

Senator SESSIONS. That is correct. We have gotten good support and worked through a lot of different suggestions. We still have some good suggestions we will wrestle with and maybe this morning we will ask some questions about them.

Chairman WARNER. I personally have worked with Secretary Rumsfeld on this issue, and I commend him for his leadership in suggesting to the administration to get out very promptly on this issue.

Dr. CHU. Thank you, Mr. Chairman.

Chairman WARNER. Thank you.

Mr. Epley, we welcome you from the Department of Veterans' Affairs. You have the title of Associate Deputy Under Secretary for Policy and Program Management, Veterans' Affairs Benefits Administration. Thank you, sir.

STATEMENT OF ROBERT J. EPLEY, ASSOCIATE DEPUTY UNDER SECRETARY FOR POLICY AND PROGRAM MANAGEMENT, VETERANS BENEFITS ADMINISTRATION, DEPARTMENT OF VETERANS' AFFAIRS

Mr. EPLEY. Good morning, Mr. Chairman. Thank you for the opportunity to testify today on this important issue. Providing benefits to survivors of our military veterans is one of our core responsibilities at the Department of Veterans' Affairs. My written testimony describes the benefits provided by VA in detail, so I will try to summarize that this morning.

The VA administers a program already alluded to today called DIC. This program pays a monthly benefit to the surviving spouse and dependent children of a veteran who died in service or as the result of a service-related disability. Currently we are paying DIC to the survivors of more than 318,000 of our veterans. Generally the monthly pay for surviving spouses is $993 per month plus $247 for each child. If the only beneficiary were a child, if there were no surviving spouse, the pay rate would be $421 for that child.

Chairman WARNER. You might mention the tax consequences also.

Mr. EPLEY. These benefits are not taxable.

Chairman WARNER. That is important to include that in the record.

Mr. EPLEY. Death pension benefits are also available for surviving spouses and unmarried minor children of deceased veterans with wartime service. Eligibility is based on financial need and is not payable to those with estates large enough to provide maintenance.

The current annual rate for a death pension for a surviving spouse with no dependents and no income is $6,814. We are currently paying death pension benefits to the survivors of over 212,000 veterans.

The VA provides casualty assistance in partnership with the DOD for survivors of servicemembers who die while on Active-Duty. VA has outlined specific outreach requirements to include coordination with the DOD, personal visits with the survivors, and assistance with their benefit claims. We have CAOs at each of our regional offices around the country, and they are responsible for maintaining close contact with their military counterparts and to do the outreach as timely as possible.

In 2002, the VA centralized all of its in-service death claims processing. This was done to improve our coordination and to expedite the process of paying those benefit claims. Our goal is to process these claims within 2 days of receipt at the VA. We are meeting that goal for many of our claims now. Sometimes it takes us a little longer if there are complicating factors.

Education is also an important benefit for our survivors, as was mentioned earlier. The VA administers educational benefits for spouses and children of veterans who died or are permanently and totally disabled as a result of a disability arising from military service. The education benefit is $803 monthly for full-time training and is graduated down based on lesser rates of training. We paid benefits for over 68,000 beneficiaries last year and most of them were pursuing college undergraduate training, although we do pay for other vocational training.

The SGLI has been mentioned extensively already today. It is a key component of our survivors' benefits package. SGLI provides low-cost term insurance protection to servicemembers through a group policy that is issued by the Prudential Life Insurance Company. When SGLI was first established in 1965, the maximum coverage was $10,000. There have been seven coverage increases since that program's inception, resulting in the current maximum coverage of $250,000. The participation rate for SGLI is 98 percent for Active-Duty members in 2004 and 93 percent for those in the Ready Reserve.

Beneficiary financial counseling services are also available through the VA Insurance Program. This is one-on-one, free, and objective counseling for SGLI beneficiaries provided by ComPsych, a vendor under contract with Prudential to help them handle the expenses and plan that expense.

There have been numerous improvements to the VA benefit package in the last few years. DIC eligibility requirements have been enhanced for surviving spouses of ex-prisoners of war (POW) and for those who remarry after the age of 57. Education payments have been significantly increased in recent years, and surviving spouses of an individual who died on Active-Duty now have 20 years to use the benefit instead of 10 years, which it was previously. Life insurance has been extended to spouses of members covered under SGLI and, as of 2001, up to $100,000 of coverage can be purchased for these spouses.

Mr. Chairman, in summary, a surviving spouse of a deceased veteran may be entitled through the VA only—there are other benefits sir—to DIC benefits of $993 a month, education benefits of $803 a month, a home loan guarantee in place of the veteran, and an insurance benefit of $250,000 and possibly other benefits as well.

The VA welcomes review and enhancement of these benefits to ensure the fair and compassionate care for survivors of our veterans, and we welcome the opportunity to work with the DOD and with this committee. I will be happy to answer any questions the committee has.

[The prepared statement of Mr. Epley follows:]

PREPARED STATEMENT BY ROBERT J. EPLEY

Mr. Chairman and members of the committee, thank you for the opportunity to testify today on this important issue. Providing benefits for survivors of our military veterans is one of our core responsibilities at the Department of Veterans' Affairs (VA).

VA provides a wide range of benefits for the surviving spouses, dependent children, and dependent parents of deceased veterans and military servicemembers. My testimony will summarize the benefits we provide, some of the recent changes to those benefits, and the scope of our payment systems. It should be noted that these are not the only death benefits a surviving spouse and children are entitled to. They are also entitled to an array of Defense and Social Security benefits that both complement and in some cases offset each other. As we examine the adequacy of these benefits, we must do so in a holistic manner.

COMPENSATION AND PENSION

One of our largest survivor programs, Dependency and Indemnity Compensation (DIC), is administered by the Compensation & Pension Service (C&P). The program pays a monthly benefit to the surviving spouse, dependent children, and dependent parents of a veteran who died in service or as the result of a service-related disability. Currently there are 318,574 cases on the C&P rolls. (A case may include more than one beneficiary, such as a spouse and minor children). DIC may also be paid when a veteran was receiving or entitled to receive VA disability compensation at the total (100 percent) disability rate for one or more service-connected disabilities for at least 10 years immediately before death, or for at least 5 years and continuously from the date of military discharge. Entitlement on this basis may be established regardless of the cause of death.

Recent legislation relating to spouses of former prisoners of war (POWs) reduced the time required for the veteran to be evaluated as totally disabled. DIC is now payable to the surviving spouse of a former POW who died after September 30, 1999, and was rated totally disabled due to service-connected conditions for a period of at least 1 year immediately preceding death. Entitlement on this basis may also be established regardless of the cause of death.

Surviving spouses of veterans who died on or after January 1, 1993, receive $993 a month. For a spouse entitled to DIC based on the veteran's death prior to January 1, 1993, the amount paid is the greater of $993 or an amount based on the veteran's pay grade. In 2001, VA completed a DIC Program Evaluation which recommended an increase in benefits for survivors with children. As a result, Congress enacted legislation last session that provides for a transitional benefit of $250 per month payable to a surviving spouse who has a minor child or children. It is payable for up to 2 years after DIC entitlement commences.

A surviving spouse who loses entitlement to DIC upon remarriage may have eligibility restored if the remarriage later ends in death, divorce, or annulment. Under Public Law 108–183, widows entitled to DIC may now retain eligibility to receive that benefit if they remarry following attainment of age 57.

Monthly DIC payments for parents of deceased veterans depend on their income. The maximum rate payable is $487 per month for a sole surviving, unremarried parent or a remarried parent living with spouse, and with income of not more than $800 per month.

Surviving spouses and unmarried children of deceased veterans with wartime service who do not qualify for DIC may be eligible for death pension benefits. Eligibility is based on financial need and is not payable to those with estates large enough to provide maintenance. The veteran must have been discharged under conditions other than dishonorable and must have had 90 days or more of active military service, at least 1 day of which was during a period of war, or have been discharged for a service-connected disability and had active military service during a period of war. If the veteran died in service but not in the line-of-duty, pension may be payable if the veteran had completed at least 2 years of honorable service.

C&P death pension cases total 212,551 as of December 2004. (A case may include more than one beneficiary, such as a spouse and minor children). The current annual rate of death pension for a surviving spouse with no dependents and no income is $6,814. Additional benefits may be available if the surviving spouse is in a nursing home, in need or regular aid and attendance, or permanently housebound. The maximum annual rate for a surviving child who is not in the custody of a surviving spouse who is eligible for death pension is $1,734. Payments are reduced by the amount of recipients' annual income from other sources, such as Social Security.

CASUALTY ASSISTANCE PROGRAM

Following the terrorist attacks of September 11, 2001, and with the start of Operation Enduring Freedom (OEF), a VA/Department of Defense (DOD) Casualty Assistance Task Group was brought together to discuss procedures for managing mass casualties and ways to improve processing of all in-service death claims. As a result, a Casualty Assistance Program was revitalized and streamlined to focus on assistance to survivors of servicemembers who die while on Active-Duty.

This program has worked effectively to streamline both the DIC application and claims-adjudication processes for survivors of servicemembers who die on Active-Duty. In addition, VA has outlined specific outreach requirements, to include personal visits with survivors. In 2002, all in-service death DIC claims were centralized to the Philadelphia Regional Office for processing. VBA casualty assistance officers (CAOs) were assigned to each regional office to work closely with military CAOs, and visit survivors to provide benefits information and assistance.

EDUCATION

Education is also an important benefit for survivors. Surviving spouses and children can gain eligibility to educational assistance based on the servicemember's death or, following Active-Duty, his or her permanent and total service-connected disability. Last year, VA paid educational assistance to 53,007 dependents of seriously disabled veterans and 15,913 survivors.

Dependents' Education Assistance (DEA) benefits are available to spouses who have not remarried and children of: (1) individuals who died on Active-Duty or are permanently and totally disabled as the result of a disability arising from active military service; (2) veterans who died from any cause while rated permanently and totally disabled from service-connected disability; (3) servicemembers listed for more than 90 days as currently missing in action or captured in line-of-duty by a hostile force; (4) servicemembers listed for more than 90 days as currently detained or interned by a foreign government or power.

The termination of a surviving spouse's remarriage, either by death or divorce, will reinstate DEA benefits to the surviving spouse. Additionally, Public Law 108–183 permits surviving spouses entitled to DEA benefits to retain those benefits if they remarry after age 57.

Benefits may be awarded for pursuit of associate, bachelor, or graduate degrees at colleges and universities, including independent study, cooperative training, and study abroad programs. Courses leading to a certificate or diploma from business, technical or vocational schools also may be taken. Benefits may also be awarded for apprenticeships, on-the-job training programs, and farm cooperative courses.

Today's monthly rate is $803 for full-time pursuit of an approved education or training program, with lesser amounts for part-time training. This benefit is available for 45 months of full time training, and payments to a spouse end 10 years from the date the individual is found eligible or from the date of the death of the veteran.

Recent legislation granted an extension in eligibility to the surviving spouse of an individual who died while on Active-Duty. They now have 20 years to use the benefit.

VA will also pay a special Montgomery GI Bill (MGIB) death benefit to a designated survivor in the event of the service-connected death of an individual while on Active-Duty or within 1 year after discharge or release. The deceased must either have been entitled to educational assistance under the MGIB program or a participant in the program who would have been so entitled but for the high school diploma or length-of-service requirement. The amount paid will be equal to the participant's actual military pay reduction, less any education benefits paid.

INSURANCE

The Servicemembers' Group Life Insurance (SGLI) program, first established in 1965, provides automatic low-cost term insurance protection to servicemembers through a group policy purchased by VA from Prudential Life Insurance Company of America. The Government pays the claim costs resulting from the extra hazards of service. All other costs of the program are covered by premiums deducted from the insured servicemember's pay.

When SGLI was first established, the maximum amount of coverage available was set at $10,000. There have been seven coverage increases since the program's inception. Recent increases include a coverage increase in 1996 when the maximum coverage available was raised from $100,000 to $200,000, and then again in 2001, when coverage was increased to the current maximum of $250,000.

Unless they decline to participate, basic SGLI coverage is automatically provided to those members on Active-Duty in the Army, Navy, Air Force, Marine Corps, and Coast Guard, as well as Reserve Officers Training Corps (ROTC) members, and uniformed members of the Public Health Service and National Oceanic and Atmospheric Administration. The Ready Reserve is also insured by SGLI, including reservists and members of the National Guard. The participation rate at the end of the 2004 Policy Year was 98 percent for Active-Duty (including reservists called to Active-Duty) and 93 percent for the Ready Reserve.

As of January 2005, the Office of Servicemembers' Group Life Insurance (OSGLI) has issued over 1,900 payments to beneficiaries as a result of 1,512 deaths certified by the branches of service in OEF and Operation Iraqi Freedom (OIF). Only ten of these members had declined SGLI coverage. Of the remaining members, 31 had opted for coverage amounts less than the maximum of $250,000. Claims paid to survivors of OIF/OEF servicemembers total over $341,857,000.

The Veterans' Survivors Benefits Improvement Act of 2001 extended life insurance coverage to spouses and children of members insured under the SGLI program, effective November 1, 2001. Spousal coverage is available to the spouses of Active-Duty servicemembers and members of the Ready Reserve of a uniformed service. Up to $100,000 of coverage can be purchased by the member for a spouse, in increments of $10,000. SGLI spousal coverage may not be greater than the amount of the servicemember's coverage. The maximum coverage for a child is $10,000.

In the case where a servicemember is married to another servicemember, the potential survivor benefit for this group of individuals is $350,000—$250,000 Basic SGLI coverage plus $100,000 Family SGLI spousal coverage. It is estimated that there are currently 84,000 such married personnel currently serving on Active-Duty.

Beneficiary Financial Counseling Services (BFCS) is one-on-one, free, objective financial counseling for SGLI beneficiaries provided by ComPsych, a vendor under contract with Prudential. Services include estate settlement and planning, investment planning, budgeting, and income tax planning. BFCS was started as a pilot project in 1999, and has now been adopted as a permanent feature of the SGLI program of benefits. Over 190 beneficiaries have taken advantage of this service since its inception.

BURIAL BENEFITS

To the extent that the DOD benefits would not cover the full amount of funeral expenses, VA is authorized to pay up to $2,000 to cover burial and funeral expenses in cases of service-connected deaths. In addition, VA provides burial in national cemeteries and also provides burial flags and markers for the graves of deceased servicemembers.

OTHER BENEFITS

In addition to the benefits described above, VA offers a range of additional benefits to survivors, including home loan guaranties, the Restored Entitlement Program, and educational or vocational counseling services.

CONCLUSION

Mr. Chairman, in summary, a surviving spouse of a deceased veteran may be entitled to basic DIC benefits of $993 per month, educational benefits of $803 per month, home loan guaranty, and an insurance benefit of $250,000.

As you can see, VA provides a substantial array of benefits to care for the survivors of servicemembers and veterans. We continue to strive toward enhanced benefits for veterans and their survivors to fulfill our mission of world class service. This completes my statement, and I will be happy to answer any questions you and other members of the committee might have.

Chairman WARNER. Thank you very much.

For those following the hearing who might not fully understand, the very important matters relating to men and women of the Armed Forces on Active-Duty and then when they go on into their next status following Active-Duty are really divided between the DOD where we have jurisdiction over the death benefit and the Veterans Benefits Administration where you have jurisdiction over other benefits. So it is a composite of two Departments of the Federal Government working together on behalf of the service persons and the veterans and their families. I think you, Dr. Chu, together with Mr. Epley, have properly framed how that responsibility is divided.

We will now turn to our distinguished military witnesses. Senator McCain, Senator Levin, others, and I, as we put together this hearing, felt it very important that, first and foremost, the military Departments be heard through the Vice Chiefs because, having had the privilege of serving the Department myself many years ago, I know full well the burdens on the Vice Chiefs and the personnel issues. While shared indeed by the Chief, often the details are left to the Vice Chiefs.

So we will turn first to the distinguished General Cody of the senior service of the United States Army. I know, General, from our talks you have, I think, two sons who currently have either been in Iraq or out of Iraq or both, proudly serving in the United States Army. Thank you.

STATEMENT OF GEN RICHARD A. CODY, USA, VICE CHIEF OF STAFF, UNITED STATES ARMY

General CODY. Thank you, Chairman Warner, Senator Levin, and distinguished members of this Senate Armed Services Committee.

We are a Nation at war. You recognize it, and our soldiers know you are behind them. I thank the members of this committee for their continued outstanding support to the men and women in uniform who make up our great Army, Active, Guard, and Reserve. Your concern, resolute action, and deep commitment to America's sons and daughters are widely recognized throughout the rank and file of our Service.

The Army is always willing to address ways to better support our soldiers and family members, especially after a loss of a soldier who was actively serving this Nation. We are very encouraged by the recent interest in raising the death gratuity and SGLI for our soldiers, and we fully support these efforts to improve compensation to the families of our fallen soldiers. Furthermore, we believe these increases should be retroactive.

Caring for survivors is a manifestation of the Army ethos to never leave a fallen comrade. The benefits and compensation due to survivors only begin with a nontaxable death gratuity, but even while there are many other forms of compensation that we have heard of today, there is still more I believe we can do. Clearly, there are voids in the system, and we are grateful to this committee for leading the effort to fill these gaps for our soldier survivors.

Everything we do to support survivors would not be possible without this committee's steadfast dedication to the military and to America's sons and daughters who are serving selflessly around the world to make America safe and free today. Every soldier's life is priceless. No benefit can replace those we have lost in the defense of this country. We owe it to our soldiers who raised their right hand and said, "America, in your time of need, send me," to make sure we get this right.

Thank you again for your continued support, and I look for the opportunity to answer all your questions.

[The prepared statement of General Cody follows:]

PREPARED STATEMENT BY GEN RICHARD A. CODY, USA

Chairman Warner, Senator Levin and distinguished members of the Senate Armed Services Committee, I would like to express our appreciation at the opportunity to appear before you to discuss soldier death gratuity and survivor benefits. I thank the members of the committee for their continued outstanding support to the men and women in uniform, who make up our great Army. Your concern, resolute action, and deep commitment to America's sons and daughters are widely recognized throughout the ranks of our Service.

Today, our over 1 million strong All-Volunteer Army is supporting the National Security Strategy with 650,000 soldiers from all components on Active-Duty. Over 300,000 of those soldiers are mobilized or deployed in 120 countries worldwide with many engaged in direct combat as we fight the war on terrorism. Increased injury and death of soldiers is an unfortunate consequence of this war.

Advanced technology and training has enabled us to improve both the protective equipment we provide to soldiers and the medical care available when the soldier is wounded. Body armor protecting the soldier's torsos is helping prevent many deaths. In previous conflicts, soldiers who would have died from massive injury to their torsos are now surviving, although many have severe wounds to their arms and legs. The current expertise of our combat medics supported by resuscitative surgical care available in forward surgical teams and combat support hospitals enable soldiers to survive these wounds. Unfortunately, many of these wounds have resulted in amputations.

Some of these soldiers, when they desire, are able to remain on Active-Duty and continue to once again contribute through their outstanding service. Sergeant First Class Luis Rodriguez, while serving in the 101st Airborne Division as a medical platoon sergeant in Iraq, lost most of his right leg. Today, he is making a difference by instructing combat life saving at Fort Campbell, Kentucky. Captain David Rozelle, from the 3rd Armored Cavalry Regiment, after losing the lower part of his right leg, has completed the Army 10-Miler and the New York City Marathon, and is back in command of his second troop unit that is going into combat with this next rotation. But not all soldiers are as fortunate as these two men, and the Army is determined to provide our disabled soldiers and families the care, support and assistance they so rightly deserve for their selfless service and sacrifice to our Nation.

Walter Reed Army Medical Center established the Army Amputee Care Program in 2001 to apply revolutionary advances in medical care and technology to the military's amputee care protocols. Through the innovative spirit of Army health care providers and through generous support of Congress we have established a state-of-the art Amputee Care Center at Walter Reed that has served as the central site for military amputee care for Operations Enduring Freedom and Iraqi Freedom (OEF/OIF). Two weeks ago, the Army Surgeon General expanded the Amputee Care Program by opening a second Amputee Care Center at Brooke Army Medical Center at Fort Sam Houston, Texas. This second site will help the Army better manage military amputees by allowing soldiers from the western half of the United States to receive treatment and rehabilitation in closer proximity to their homes.

On April 30, 2004, the Department of the Army introduced a Disabled Soldier Support System (DS3) Initiative that provides its severely disabled soldiers and their families with a system of advocacy and follow-up with personal support to assist them as they confront the stress of their wounds and think through the difficult decision of continuing to pursue a military career or transitioning from military service to the civilian community. Working closely with the Joint Support Operations Center, DS3 incorporates and integrates several existing programs to provide holistic support services for our severely disabled soldiers and their families throughout their phased progression from initial casualty notification to their return to home station and final career disposition. The system facilitates communication and coordination between severely disabled soldiers and their families and the pertinent local, Federal and national agencies and organizations, such as the Department of Veterans' Affairs (VA) and the many commendable Veterans Service Organizations. In addition, DS3 will utilize a system to track and monitor severely disabled soldiers for a period of up to 5 years beyond their medical retirement in order to provide appropriate assistance through an array of existing service providers.

Regrettably, despite our great lifesaving systems and best efforts, the Army has soldiers who die for reasons ranging from enemy fire to natural causes and we must address this reality in periods of peace and war.

Regardless of the cause of death, when one of our soldiers dies it is a tragic loss for the soldier's survivors. Having addressed the difficult issue of compensating survivors throughout the Army's history, we know very well that no benefit can replace a human life. Although there is no substitute for a fallen soldier's survivors, we are committed to doing all we can to assist them during their period of loss and beyond. Caring for survivors is a manifestation of our ethos to never leave a fallen comrade, and one way the Army lives up to this commitment is through our Casualty Assistance Program.

When a soldier dies, a Casualty Assistance Officer (CAO) stays with the family following notification of their loss. Families have access to their CAO during the days, weeks, months, and, sometimes, even years after their servicemember's death. These officers provide valuable counsel and support to the families, offering the family important advice, running interference when problems arise, arranging for the military funeral, and ensuring that the families receive all services and compensation due them. The services and compensation due to survivors include:

DEATH GRATUITY

A $12,420 nontaxable death gratuity is intended to provide immediate cash to meet the needs of survivors. In general, the death gratuity is payable immediately upon the death of a soldier.

SERVICEMEMBERS' GROUP LIFE INSURANCE

Soldiers may elect insurance coverage in multiples of $10,000 up to a maximum coverage of $250,000 under the Servicemembers' Group Life Insurance (SGLI) Program. SGLI is a Government group life insurance program providing coverage to soldiers at rates often lower than those available, given the added risk in insuring members of the Armed Forces, under normal commercial insurance policies.

UNPAID PAY AND ALLOWANCES

Unpaid pay and allowances are payable to designated beneficiary to include accrued leave.

DEPENDENCY AND INDEMNITY COMPENSATION

The VA pays this tax-free monthly benefit to an unremarried surviving spouse of a soldier who dies from a service-connected disability and to the soldier's dependent children and parents. The basic spousal Dependency and Indemnity Compensation (DIC) is currently $993 per month. An additional $247 per month is payable to the spouse for each dependent child of the deceased soldier under the age of 18. Additional amounts are authorized for specific purposes. Spouse eligibility for DIC ends upon remarriage before age 58. DIC can be restored if the remarriage ends in death or divorce.

Surviving spouses and unmarried children of deceased veterans with wartime service who do not qualify for DIC may be eligible for death pension benefits. Eligibility is based on financial need and is not payable to those with estates large enough to provide maintenance. The veteran must have been discharged under conditions other than dishonorable and must have had 90 days or more of active military service, at least one day of which was during a period of war, or have been discharged for a service-connected disability and had active military service during a period of war. If the veteran died in service but not in the line-of-duty, pension may be payable if the veteran had completed at least 2 years of honorable service.

SURVIVOR BENEFIT PLAN (SBP)

Surviving spouses of soldiers who die on Active-Duty are entitled to monthly annuity payments under the SBP. If there is no surviving spouse, dependent children are eligible. Also eligible is a former spouse of a soldier who has been ordered by a state court to enroll the former spouse in SBP at retirement. The amount of the annuity for a surviving spouse under age 62 is 55 percent of the retired pay the soldier would have been entitled to receive if the soldier had applied for retirement on the date of death. The amount of the annuity for a surviving spouse age 62 or older is currently 35 percent (DIC offset) until October 2005 when it becomes 40 percent and is gradually tiered to 55 percent by April 2008. There is no DIC/SBP offset applicable to children. A surviving spouse who remarries before reaching age 55 loses entitlement to SBP, although SBP is reinstated if the remarriage ends in death or divorce.

SOCIAL SECURITY

Social Security death benefits are payable on behalf of a "currently insured" deceased soldier to a surviving spouse caring for the deceased soldier's dependent children under age 16 and to eligible minor children of the deceased soldier. Social Security old-age survivor benefits are payable on behalf of a "fully insured" deceased soldier to a surviving spouse at least 60 years old. The amount of an old age survivor benefit is a percentage of a deceased Soldier's Primary Insurance Amount, and depends on the age of the survivor at the time of applying for a Social Security old age survivor benefit.

VA DEPENDENTS' EDUCATION ASSISTANCE

Dependents' Education Assistance (DEA) benefits are available to spouses who have not remarried and children of: (1) individuals who died on Active-Duty or are permanently and totally disabled as the result of a disability arising from active military service; (2) veterans who died from any cause while rated permanently and totally disabled from service-connected disability; (3) servicemembers listed for more than 90 days as currently missing in action or captured in line of duty by a hostile force; (4) servicemembers listed for more than 90 days as currently detained or interned by a foreign government or power. This benefit is available for 45 months of full time training, and payments to a spouse end 10 years from the date the individual is found eligible or from the date of the death of the veteran. Children have until their 26th birthday to use their education benefits.

SERVICE ACADEMY PREFERENCE

Children of soldiers who die on Active-Duty (are missing in action or who die as a result of a disability rated 100 percent) receive Academy preference for appointment in order of merit by competitive examination.

MONTGOMERY GI BILL (TITLE 38)

VA will pay a special Montgomery GI Bill (MGIB) death benefit to a designated survivor in the event of a service-connected death of a soldier while on Active-Duty or within 1 year after discharge or release. The soldier's survivor must apply through the VA.

HEALTH CARE

A surviving spouse less than 65 years old and the minor dependents of a deceased soldier are eligible for space-available medical care at military medical treatment facilities or are otherwise covered by TRICARE. A surviving spouse 65 years old or older is eligible for space-available medical care at military medical treatment facilities (MTFs) or is otherwise covered by Medicare and TRICARE-for-Life. In certain very uncommon situations when survivors of those who die in service are not eligible for military medical benefits, VA's CHAMPVA Program will provide them with medical benefits.

FAMILY MEMBER DENTAL PLAN

A surviving spouse of a soldier and dependents are eligible to enroll in a Family Member Dental Plan for a period of 1 year when the soldier dies on Active-Duty and the dependents were enrolled prior to the death of the soldier.

COMMISSARY AND EXCHANGE PRIVILEGES

The unmarried surviving spouse and qualified dependents of a deceased soldier are eligible to shop at military commissaries and exchanges.

THEATER AND RECREATION FACILITIES

The unmarried surviving spouse and qualified dependents of a deceased soldier are eligible to utilize theater and recreation facilities.

TAX BENEFITS

The next-of-kin of a deceased soldier whose death occurs overseas in a terrorist or military action is exempt from paying Federal income tax on income received by the decedent during the year of the decedent's death.

CONTINUED GOVERNMENT HOUSING OR AN ALLOWANCE IN LIEU THEREOF

Survivors are provided rent-free Government housing for 180 days after the death of a soldier or a tax-free housing allowance for that portion of the 180-day period not in Government housing, with the amount of the allowance based on the soldier's grade at the time of death.

GUARANTEED HOUSING LOANS

Surviving spouses of servicemembers who died on Active-Duty from a service-connected disability or of veterans who died from a service-connected disability are granted VA housing loan benefits. This allows surviving spouses to obtain home loans on favorable terms without the need to make a down payment.

BURIAL COST AND CARE OF REMAINS OF SOLDIER

The DOD reimburses expenses for the soldier's burial, depending on the type of arrangements, and provides travel for next-of-kin under invitational travel orders in an amount not larger than normally incurred by the Secretary in furnishing the supply or service concerned. To the extent that the DOD benefits would not cover the full amount of funeral expenses, VA is authorized to pay up to $2,000 to cover burial and funeral expenses in cases of service-connected deaths. In addition, VA provides burial in national cemeteries and also provides burial flags and markers for the graves of deceased servicemembers.

BURIAL ALLOWANCE PAYABLE BY SOCIAL SECURITY

Limited to those who have surviving dependents, it pays $255 in one lump sum to the spouse. If no surviving spouse, it is paid to children who are eligible to draw Social Security benefits.

GRAVE AND MEMORIAL MARKERS

Headstones and markers are provided by VA for the graves of those interred in private, local, State veterans, or National Cemeteries without charge and shipped at Government expense to the consignee designated. The cost of placing a marker in a State, local, or private cemetery must be born by the applicant.

BURIAL IN NATIONAL CEMETERY

Soldiers who die while in active military, naval, or air service are eligible for burial in a National Cemetery. Space may also be reserved for a spouse. Minor/handicapped children of such soldiers may also be buried in National/Post Cemetery.

MILITARY FUNERAL

Soldiers who die while on Active-Duty are eligible for a military funeral. The CAO coordinates the funeral with the Army installation responsible for the geographic area where the interment is to take place.

SHIPMENT OF PERSONAL EFFECTS

When a soldier dies on Active-Duty, his or her personal effects are shipped to the place of residence of the authorized recipient, if the recipient did not reside with the deceased soldier.

TRAVEL OF DEPENDENTS AND SHIPMENT OF HOUSEHOLD GOODS AND PERSONAL EFFECTS AT GOVERNMENT EXPENSE

The spouse and dependent children of a soldier that dies may move one time at Government expense. Household goods will not be moved a greater distance than the personal travel. One motor vehicle can be shipped at Government expense.

OTHER VA BENEFITS

VA also offers a range of additional benefits to survivors, including home loan guaranties, the Restored Entitlement Program, and educational or vocational counseling services.

While there are many forms of compensation, there is still more that we can do. Clearly there are voids in the system, and we are grateful for the numerous organizations that step-up to fill the gaps in support of soldiers' survivors. Countless charitable organizations are providing an invaluable link between the American people and surviving families to channel support. Through large organizations such as the Intrepid Foundation's Fallen Heroes Fund and numerous less well-known organizations and individuals, the American people are making a difference. Whether in the form of financial support, counseling, or other services, these organizations and their supporters untiringly communicate the American people's support for their fallen. As our All-Volunteer Force continues to stand strong in its most challenging hour, the contributions of these charitable organizations are absolutely invaluable to the well being of our force. We cannot thank them enough.

The Army is always willing to address ways to better support our family members, especially after the loss of a soldier who was actively serving our Nation. We are very encouraged by recent interest in raising the death gratuity and other survivor benefits for our soldiers and will support any efforts to improve compensation to the families of our fallen.

Everything we do to support survivors would not be possible without this committee's steadfast dedication to your military and to America's sons and daughters, who are serving selflessly throughout the world to make America safe and free. Thank you and your committee for your continued support of our soldiers and their families and for your leadership in providing better survivor benefits. Thank you again for this opportunity to discuss issues surrounding support to our severely wounded soldiers as well as the death gratuity and survivor benefits. I look forward to the opportunity to participate in this session and answering any questions you may have.

Chairman WARNER. Thank you. You said retroactive. If you have set a date, I missed it.

General CODY. I have not set a date, sir. I think that will be part of the discussion.

Chairman WARNER. It will be part of the discussion.

General CODY. Yes, sir.

Chairman WARNER. So you purposely omitted reference to a date.

General CODY. Yes, sir.

Chairman WARNER. Thank you.

From the United States Navy, Admiral Nathman.

STATEMENT OF ADM JOHN B. NATHMAN, USN, VICE CHIEF OF NAVAL OPERATIONS, UNITED STATES NAVY

Admiral NATHMAN. Thank you, Mr. Chairman, Senator Levin, and the distinguished members of this committee. Thank you for the opportunity to address you here today to discuss the support and assistance we provide to our surviving family members and for the care of our severely injured sailors, soldiers, marines, and airmen.

This is clearly a subject worthy of our collective time and debate, and for those of us serving, we are thankful for your attention to this important matter. We appreciate the continuing support, both in policy and in resources, that enables us to provide a continuum of care for our servicemembers. Your efforts here today, just deliberating this issue, signals your clear concern to our servicemembers and their families.

I also appreciate this committee's efforts in working with other committees of Congress to ensure the appropriate balance of benefits and the capabilities to meet the needs of the armed servicemember. I particularly appreciated the way Senator Sessions put it. I believe there is a very strong bond between the citizens of the United States and those who serve in uniform. That bond is strong. I would call it a covenant bond. I think if we are going to talk about benefits for those who serve, it should not be just for those who are in a designated geographic area.

So I look forward to working with you and your staffs as we move forward and will remain fully engaged and committed in delivering the right benefits on behalf of a grateful Nation. Thank you, sir.

[The prepared statement of Admiral Nathman follows:]

PREPARED STATEMENT BY ADM JOHN B. NATHMAN, USN

INTRODUCTION

Mr. Chairman, Senator Levin, members of this distinguished committee, thank you for the opportunity to be here today to discuss the ongoing support and assistance we provide our surviving family members and the care provided for our severely injured sailors. Providing this support and care to our sailors and their families is a Navy priority and each case is handled individually by a trained professional.

NAVY CASUALTY ASSISTANCE

These deliberations today are both important and serious. We go to great lengths to recruit and train our servicemembers and to welcome them and their families into the great tradition and heritage of the United States Navy. Members of the Armed Forces may give their lives while serving our country in the line-of-duty. When a sailor dies, our sole mission is to render prompt and compassionate assistance to help reduce the suffering of the servicemember's family. We have a casualty assistance network available 24/7, a group of highly dedicated and trained professionals that notify the next of kin as fast as possible and then remain with them during the weeks ahead. These Casualty Assistance Calls Officers (CACO), who are customarily accompanied by a Navy chaplain, make all notifications in person. The Navy's highly effective program is staffed by specially selected senior enlisted and officers who are well suited to effectively perform this difficult task.

The CACO's full time responsibility is to support the family. The CACO will assist with funeral preparations; travel to and from a burial site; and attend the burial service. The CACO assists the family with various claims to obtain their benefits and entitlements as well as any relocation desires. Supporting the CACO are Regional Casualty Coordinators and headquarters personnel who personally supervise each case to ensure that all families are accorded the highest level of attention and assistance. As you might imagine, the needs of individual families vary dramatically, but the assigned CACO attempts to anticipate and react expeditiously to any issue or concern that may arise. This is a well-executed program, and I am proud of our CACOs and their selfless devotion to Navy families.

SURVIVOR BENEFITS AND ENTITLEMENTS

As I mentioned, the CACO assists each family in obtaining the full financial support to which they are entitled. Navy centrally manages the processing of all death benefits and entitlements. Certification proceeds at a good pace. A death gratuity payment is made to the designated beneficiary as soon as possible following notification of the member's death. Accrued unpaid pays and allowances owed to the member, to include any unused leave, reenlistment bonus installments, uniform allowances, etc., are generally paid within 7 to 10 days. Payment of Servicemember Group Life Insurance (SGLI) generally occurs within 7 to 10 days. Basic Allowance for Housing (BAH) is generally paid within 30 days. Payment of Dependency Indemnity Compensation (DIC) from the Department of Veterans' Affairs (VA) is paid within 6–8 weeks and the Survivor Benefit Plan (SBP) annuities are also paid within 6–8 weeks. I want to add that Navy truly appreciates the strategic partnerships formed with the VA and Social Security Administration (SSA) to expedite benefits processing partnerships that have streamlined submissions and greatly increased processing efficiencies. I would like to mention that there are times, however, when this process is temporarily—and consciously—halted in order to protect the interests of a family member. For example, in the case of a minor child named as a beneficiary; we must wait until a legal guardian is appointed before making payment. These cases are not systemic problems, but systemic protections for the individual receiving benefits.

The Navy also counsels and encourages our surviving family members to utilize the financial counseling offered by the Office of Servicemembers' Group Life Insurance (OSGLI) as well as grief counseling offered by the VA, both of which have proven reliable and available free of charge.

MEDICAL CARE AND SUPPORT OF OUR CRITICALLY INJURED

The Navy also has a coordinated and tailored response for the men and women of our Armed Forces returning from Iraq, Afghanistan, and other areas of conflict with severe debilitating injuries. These servicemembers and their families are faced with very difficult long-term challenges. The Navy and Marine Corps team provides a strong coordinated and unified approach to assist them and their families to recover and reintegrate.

Our patients and their families deserve excellent health care. Severely wounded sailors and marines are almost always transferred from overseas to National Naval Medical Center (NNMC) in Bethesda for care. NNMC representatives meet with all incoming medical evaluation (MEDEVAC) patients and family members upon their arrival. Patients are admitted and surgical and/or medical teams make further medical assessments and establish the best course of treatment.

Planning for post-hospital care begins almost immediately upon arrival at Bethesda. Because family support is essential to the recovery of injured servicemembers, the Navy takes full advantage of all resources afforded to them and maximizes these in developing the most appropriate care plan for their recovery and rehabilitation. Depending on the specific needs of the sailor and marine, their care plans could include care at another military treatment facility (MTF), a Veterans' Medical Center, or in some cases a specialized civilian facility.

Some examples of our integrated health care delivery team include the coordination between the NNMC Social Work and Case Management Departments, counselors from the VA, and the Marine Corps Liaison Office—all located on the Bethesda campus. Representatives from these organizations interact with patients and family members throughout the course of treatment. They serve as educators for their respective programs and advocates for the needs of the patient and their families.

Our goal is for every patient to return to Active-Duty. Some of those who are injured, and placed in a limited duty status, go on to receive specialized care only available through the VA. These servicemembers remain on Active-Duty and are closely monitored by Navy Medicine. Other sailors or marines, who have fully recovered, but sustained permanent injuries, may seek waiver status to remain on Active-Duty, and receive their care at MTFs. Regrettably, some servicemembers have sustained injuries that will prevent them from remaining on Active-Duty. In these cases, the patients and their families are supported to the fullest extent possible as they transition to veteran's status under the VA.

CONCLUSION

Chairman Warner, I thank you and the members of this committee for your continued support and the opportunity to appear before the full committee today. All of us serving in the Armed Forces are thankful for your attention to this important matter.

Chairman WARNER. Thank you, Admiral Nathman. We welcome you. I believe this is your first appearance before the full committee.

Admiral NATHMAN. Yes, sir.

Chairman WARNER. You will be back.

Admiral NATHMAN. Thank you, sir. [Laughter.]

Chairman WARNER. General Nyland.

STATEMENT OF GEN. WILLIAM L. NYLAND, USMC, ASSISTANT COMMANDANT, UNITED STATES MARINE CORPS

General NYLAND. Thank you, Mr. Chairman, Senator Levin, distinguished members of the committee. I appreciate the opportunity to address you today to provide my perspective on these vital issues associated with the care of our war casualties and their families that come as a result of their death or injury. Let me open by offering each of you and your staffs my deepest appreciation for the financial and moral support you have continuously provided to our men and women in uniform.

As marines, we pride ourselves on taking care of our own, and we work very hard to mitigate the terrible tragedy of death or disabling injury. We have very efficient internal support services to assist families in their decisionmaking and, in the case of the wounded, to help immediate family members in their travel to Bethesda, Walter Reed, or whatever facility their loved one might be hospitalized. This is the right thing to do considering their sacrifice, and it is critical to the recovery process. Your support in that in last year's act is greatly appreciated.

Not long ago, we instituted our Marine for Life program to ensure marines returning to civilian life were assisted in that transition and to nurture and sustain, once a marine, always a marine. Just recently, we have added a new aspect to the program, the Injured Support Program, which will focus on serving our disabled marines. This project is designed to help them with job search, schooling, and generally settling back into society. As you well know, it is often very difficult to navigate the complicated rules, regulations, and justifications associated with big service related organizations. We hope to help them cut that red tape, get what the law says they deserve, and what they have earned in service to this great Nation.

In this regard, we will place liaison officers with the VA and other organizations to facilitate the process. This initiative will have marines on the other end of the phone and in their communities helping marines and sailors who were injured while serving with marines.

We are here today to talk about the benefits we give the families of those who pay the ultimate price on our behalf. I do not know what the complete right answer is, but my sense is that what we receive or give them today is inadequate, and it certainly seems more than appropriate to do more to try and mitigate the loss of a loved one.

Certainly Senator Sessions' proposed HEROES Act and multiple other bills and the DOD's approach go a long way toward addressing this need. That said, I would worry that we would try and distinguish between types of service to this great Nation, be it direct combat or not. I firmly believe that we would do great harm to our service men and women, all of whom serve our great Nation magnificently, if we were to make such distinctions in one's service. Whatever we as a Nation do in the long run, we must all work together to develop benefits that assist the families of those who lose a loved one or have a severely disabled member.

Mr. Chairman, this entire committee and you personally have done so much for the casualties of this war and for their families. I know each of you feel those losses personally, and you have all made it part of your life's work to understand the plight of the families left behind.

I am honored to be here today. I look forward to working with the committee and with the Department and also to your questions. Thank you, sir.

[The prepared statement of General Nyland follows:]

PREPARED STATEMENT BY GEN. WILLIAM L. NYLAND, USMC

Chairman Warner, Senator Levin, distinguished members of the committee; today, America is at war. The Marine Corps as an institution is fully committed to this life-and-death struggle, and in protecting the American people and our way of life. The over 35,000 marines and sailors serving today in Iraq and Afghanistan are performing superbly due to their training and extraordinary courage. They, more than any of us sitting protected in this great hall today, fully understand the danger to the Nation and what it takes to ensure its survival. We can never forget there is a terrible, but necessary, human cost that cannot be measured in dollars—it is their sacrifice that we can only stand in awe of, particularly when they did not have to serve in the first place. Marines, and sailors who serve with marines, and their families, are fully aware that if you are wearing the precious Eagle, Globe and Anchor today you are either in on the field of battle, just returning, or packing your seabag to go. Since our Nation suffered the monstrous attack on September 11, 2001, 414 marines have been killed protecting every one of us here today, and nearly 4,000 have been wounded. On behalf of every marine, and the brave sailors who serve with us, their spouses, children, mothers and fathers, I thank this Congress for your continued and indispensable support. I thank the committee for the opportunity to participate in evolving efforts to insure that our protectors, regardless of uniform, and their families are provided for whether they are killed or maimed in the defense of this great Nation. I would like to begin by framing measures the Marine Corps is undertaking to reduce stress on the force and your marines and their families.

REDUCING STRESS ON THE FORCE

Currently, the Corps is fully engaged across the spectrum of military operations in prosecuting the global war on terrorism. Since the watershed events of September 11, 2001, the core competencies, capabilities, and our 50-year, nonnegotiable focus on readiness and our culture of deployment has served us well in this war. There is no operation, no trick, no new tactic or technique, regardless of how illegal or despicable, that our enemy has employed against us that we have not been able to adjust to. The high state of training and quality of our marines along with their warrior ethos—highlighted by our creed that every marine is a rifleman—allows Marines to thrive in the chaotic, unstable, and unpredictable environment that has always characterized warfare and that our very adaptable enemies methodically attempt to exploit. We took advantage of the lessons we learned during our first 10 months in Iraq—when Baghdad and Tikrit were liberated, and we administered the southern half of the country in Phase IV operations—amidst a growing insurgency, improvised explosive devices (IEDs), and criminal acts against us in the name of extremism, to prepare for our return a year ago to the Al Anbar Province where we are locked in combat today.

Since March last year, the I Marine Expeditionary Force (I MEF) of over 30,000 has fought the insurgency to a standstill in unconventional operations across the zone, as well as in bitter street fighting in Fallujah and Ramadi. With one hand stretched out in friendship to the majority of the Iraqi people who are the true victims of the extremists, and the other with weapon firmly in hand, we have endeavored to bring stability and security to the Province. Our expeditious and innovative pre-deployment combat skills training program, rapid modifications of our equipment to meet an evolving threat, and our emphasis on cultural appreciation and language capabilities, have all contributed to our considerable accomplishments in this complex region. Reinforced by three Marine Expeditionary Units (MEUs), I MEF is executing any number of security, urban combat, nation building, counterinsurgency, aviation command and control, and force protection missions with great confidence and skill. The enemy is smart, adaptable, and plays by no rule that civilized men and women would recognize; we, however, are smarter, more adaptable, and will ultimately win because our efforts are in the interests of precious liberties enshrined in our most revered national documents. Battles like those in Fallujah, Ramadi, and the Northern Babil Province link this generation of marines to the rich legacy of selfless courage and warfighting excellence, that has defined marines of every generation.

In Afghanistan this past spring, we provided, on short-notice, a regimental headquarters, an infantry battalion, and a combined arms MEU. This Marine Force was a major portion of the combined joint task force "Spring Offensive" to help set the conditions for the successful election that has advanced the process of establishing a secure and stable government in Afghanistan. We continue to provide both ground and aviation forces—currently an infantry battalion, elements of two helicopter squadrons, and training teams—to protect and foster this new democracy.

In addition to these operations, our concurrent support to other regions including the Horn of Africa, the Pacific, South Asian Tsunami relief, evacuation of noncombatants from Liberia, and the peace operation in Haiti, all has demonstrated the almost unlimited range of readiness and adaptability resident in this Corps of Marines that typically come from the sea, and return with the mission accomplished.

As on many occasions in the past, naval forces, led by marines ashore, responded quickly and were deeply involved in the saving of lives and providing comfort to millions in the wake of the Sumatran earthquake and Indian Ocean tsunami. We should not underestimate the importance of these kinds of humanitarian missions as they are not only what decent people do, but are the purest and most giving form of engagement in a region critical to the war against extremism. As an aside, the marines involved in this relief operation have re-embarked on their amphibious ships, and are back on their way to their original destination—Iraq.

Currently, we are also conducting a major rotation of our units and headquarters in Iraq. Most of these units have previously deployed to the war, but we have matched their training and equipment to take advantage of the lessons learned by those on the ground today at such a high price. The combatant commander has requested a force of nearly 22,000 marines organized around 6 maneuver battalions, 3,000 of whom are activated from our Reserve component.

While our readiness remains acceptable in the short term, the demand on the force is straining our marines, their families, and our equipment and materiel stocks. Operational tempo is high—the entire Marine Corps is supporting the global war on terror and no forces have been fenced. In the past 2 years, we have gone from a deployment rotation of one-to-three (66 months out/18 months back) to our current one-to-one ratio (7 months out/7 months back) for our infantry battalions and other high demand assets. This means that units in the operating forces are either deployed or are training to relieve deployed units. Since September 11, we have activated in excess of 95 percent of our Selected Marine Corps Reserve units. The vast majority has served in either Iraq or Afghanistan. Despite this high operational tempo, the Marine Corps continues to meet its recruiting and retention goals in quantity and quality, but the effort required by individual recruiters and career retention specialists has increased exponentially.

End Strength

We truly appreciate authorization to increase our end strength by 3,000 in the fiscal year 2005 bill. These additional marines will assist in reducing stress on the individuals already shouldering such a heavy burden. We are looking hard as to whether a further increase will be necessary to meet long-term commitments where we are fighting today, and for what might come tomorrow. We have also conducted a thorough review of internal manpower policies and procedures, completely reexamined the force structure, and have made recommendations to the Commandant on unit activation and deactivation, "civilianization," and a number of realignments. One immediate result of this effort has been the recommendation to create additional high demand units, and specialties to address pressures within the force. We are also enhancing the manning of our infantry units, creating a dedicated Foreign Military Training Unit, adding to our recruiting force, our training base, and other support for the operating forces. These initiatives, coupled with those implemented as part of the overall force structure reduce somewhat the personnel tempo and consequently of operations. It also reduces the stress on individual marines and their families.

Force Structure Review Group

As mentioned previously we recognized the need to continue transforming and rebalancing forces to meet the needs of the 21st century. A comprehensive review of our Total Force structure, Active and Reserve, was conducted last summer. We are implementing the recommended force structure initiatives with the majority achieving operational capability in fiscal year 2006, and full operational capability by fiscal year 2008. These initiatives are end strength and structure neutral—offsets to balance these increases in capabilities are internal to the Marine Corps and come from military to civilian conversions and the disestablishment and reorganization of less critical capabilities. The Marine Corps will continue to evaluate our force structure to ensure that it provides the needed capabilities in a timely manner to support our national security requirements.

Major structural changes in the active component include the establishment of two additional infantry battalions, three light armored reconnaissance companies, three reconnaissance companies, two force reconnaissance platoons, and an additional Air-Naval Gunfire Liaison Company (ANGLICO). We will also augment our existing explosive ordnance disposal, intelligence, aviation support, civil affairs, command and control, and psychological operations assets.

In the Reserve component these structure initiatives will increase the capability of Marine Forces Reserve Command as it takes an increasingly active role in the war. We will establish an Intelligence Support Battalion, a Security/Anti-terrorism Battalion, and two additional light armored reconnaissance companies. We will also augment existing capabilities in the areas of civil affairs and command and control, and we are restructuring some Reserve units to convert them into Individual Mobilization Augmentee (IMA) Detachments—allowing the Nation more timely access to these Marine reservists to support contingency operations. In terms of military to civilian conversion we continue to pursue a sensible strategy to increase the number of marines in the operating forces. Last year we converted 664 billets, and we are on course to achieve an additional 1,697 through September 2006.

Marine Corps Reserve

Thanks to strong congressional support in the past, the Marine Corps has trained and equipped its Reserve to be capable of rapid activation, and deployment. This capability allows Reserve combat deployments to mirror those of the active component in duration. These reduced duration deployments have helped us to sustain the Reserve Force, and avoid untimely extensions. Through this process, the Marine Corps has been able to maximize force management of the Reserve, maintain unit integrity, and lessen the burden on the families by maintaining generally shorter deployments.

Over 10,000 Marine Reserves are currently serving on Active-Duty in support of the war. Well over 8,000 are serving in cohesive ground, aviation, and combat support units, led by combat capable Reserve officers and noncommissioned officers (NCOs). Another 1,500 are individual augmentees in both Marine and Joint commands and headquarter elements. A total of almost 30,000 of our Reserve marines have served on Active-Duty since that terrible day in September nearly 4 years ago, with 95 percent of the units in our Reserve component having been activated.

REDUCING STRESS ON THE MARINE AND THEIR FAMILIES

The Marine Corps continues to answer the call because of our individual marines, and the support they receive from their families and from the Nation. Morale and commitment are high. Marines join the Corps to "fight and win battles" and we are certainly giving them the opportunity to do that. We are an expeditionary force accustomed to deployments, but as earlier stated, this fight is not without its costs to both marines and their families.

Marine Corps Community Services

Taking care of marines and their families is essential to the operational readiness of the Corps. The relevance of this mission is particularly evident when leaders at all levels assess preparedness of their command and unit functioning before, during, and after forward deployments. As an expeditionary force we are accustomed to frequent deployments—it is part of our culture and is one of the key reasons why young Americans join the Marine Corps—yet the current environment contains elements of personal danger and family risk that must be addressed with appropriate and timely support. To date in all our worldwide operations, we have been careful to closely monitor our programs, adjusting as needed to ensure marines and their families receive the necessary care to sustain them through every deployment cycle. In this regard, the Marine Corps Community Services (MCCS) organizations' combined structure of family services, Morale, Welfare and Recreation Programs, voluntary off duty education, and exchange operations, allow us to efficiently and effectively help families meet the challenges associated with our lifestyle and current operational tempo.

Deployment Support

During the pre-deployment period, families attend to the administrative details of wills, powers of attorney, and insurance, and family care plans, as they always have. Spouses then connect in both a formal and informal way through the commander's Key Volunteer Network organized to provide accurate and timely information on the status of the deployment. This network also mobilizes to embrace those families who receive the dreaded knock on the door to notify them of the death, or serious injury, of their loved one serving overseas. This is in addition, of course, to the formal assist provided by the casualty officer assigned in every case. The spouses involved in this program are all volunteers, work day and night without respite, and shoulder their own burdens of stress and often grief, while helping others through theirs. They are the behind-the-scenes heroes of this war, and we love them for what they do.

We have developed a series of pre-deployment, in-theater (Iraq and Afghanistan), return and reunion, and post-deployment awareness and support services to mitigate potential problems shaped by traumatic combat experiences and associated stress. The assumption we make is that none of us are immune from the social tragedies of suicide, domestic violence, or sexual assault. We also assume that risk factors can be exacerbated by a wide range of factors associated with normal deployments and most especially war, and we have implemented a variety of active counseling services to address individual and unit concerns. Examples include: the Critical Incident Stress Debriefing Program, designed to address the symptoms and risks of untreated combat stress, its signs, and the resources available for treatment; and our Operational Stress Control and Readiness Program (OSCAR), where we embed a mental health professional(s) in battalion aid stations. It has resulted in a marked decrease in evacuations for mental health reasons. Prior to departing a combat zone, and immediately upon return to home station, we have instituted a rest and decompression period in which small unit commanders, NCOs, and chaplains, provide the a Warrior Transition Brief. This series of discussions focuses on preparing returning marines and sailors to integrate with loved ones and society. A wide array of services is also available at our installations through chaplains, medical treatment facilities, and MCCS, to support every member of the marine community in the post-deployment phase of their lives. For those in need residing a distance from our installations, face-to-face counseling services are available through the MCCS OneSource Program.

We recognize that family readiness is integral to unit readiness. To help our families through the separation and stress of deployment Congress, through Supplemental Appropriations, has provided extended childcare services, and we are grateful for this support. Information and referral services are offered via different access points to include the key volunteers, command Web sites and hotlines, and MCCS OneSource, which offers round the clock information and referral services via toll-free telephone and Internet access. This program has also proven to be an especially valuable resource to assist Reserve marines and their families who often experience special challenges as they attempt to acclimate to Active-Duty life when called up.

Casualty Assistance

Every one of us, particularly the families, appreciate recent legislative actions that help in the event of a death of serious injury. In particular are those funds provided for expanded authorization for parents of our deceased to attend funerals when they are not the primary next-of-kin, and also for paid travel to the bedside of the badly injured, those facing extended hospital and rehabilitation stays. This is important to their morale, and critical in the recovery of these heroes. We have established internal support services, including an extensive network of Casualty Assistance Calls Officers (CACOs) throughout the country, that serve as the primary point of contact for the families of deceased and severely injured marines. We have always done it this way, but it's better than it has ever been as we serve these families with a shoulder to lean on, and, when it is time and they are ready for help and advice in navigating through the complexities of military benefit and entitlement programs, and even with offers from benevolent organizations who want to help. This support is managed through our Headquarters Casualty Affairs section, and has been enhanced by the development and implementation of an Office of the Secretary of Defense-funded Injured/Ill Patient Tracking Web site. Commanders now have nearly real time visibility of their injured marines through all stages in the medical and convalescence process.

In this vein, I would like to thank Congress for the continued support of the programs and services so critical to the readiness of our Corps, to include provisions of supplemental appropriations; all of which directly contribute to quality of life enhancements. Also, for your kind and caring visits at hospitals and in homes across the country, visits that provide comfort and motivation to those wounded in the war that is protecting us here at home in our daily lives.

Marine For Life—Injured Support

Building on to the organizational network and strengths of the previously established Marine for Life Program, we are currently implementing an Injured Support Program to assist the disabled after they are discharged. The goal is to never forget them or what they have done, and to bridge the often difficult and lengthy gap between the care we in the Marine Corps and Navy provide, and that which the Department of Veterans' Affairs (VA) assumes. The key is to ensure continuity of support through transition and assistance for however long it might take, and certainly to cover the gap in entitlements that sometimes is many months long. Planned features of the program include advocacy within the Marine Corps and Navy for the disabled and their families, and help getting over the hurdles of any external agencies they might interact with. An extremely big part of this will be both pre- and post-service separation case management, assistance in working with physical evaluation boards, an interactive Web site for disability/benefit information, assistance with Federal hiring preferences and law, and improved VA handling of marine cases by the attachment of a liaison officer embedded within the VA headquarters. The program began operations in early January, and it will never stop evolving and improving its services. If there is any area that needs more interest, it is in the long term help and assistance for our disabled personnel and their families.

Death Benefits

The final topic I must address is perhaps the most difficult, the death of a serviceman or woman in the defense of our way of life. While their deaths, whether it is in combat or in a training accident here in the United States, are tragic, they are heroes . . . not victims. They stepped forward to a life of service when they did not have to, and even as young as they are, they knew what they were getting into, what the dangers were, what the possibilities might be. There are those who might not believe this, but it is true. The only experience they cannot imagine, because it is unimaginable, is combat itself. They stood tall when the country needed them, came when they did not have to, and had they not, no one would call them coward. Let me walk you through what happens when a family is notified of a death.

When they open the door a marine officer is always standing there to give them the most dreaded news they will ever receive. Details are few and will typically only include the time and place of the death, and perhaps a little bit of the how. This officer then quite literally becomes part of the family for as long as they need him—forever if necessary. When appropriate, and it is always awkward, he provides them a death gratuity check for $12,000, then helps them through the process of making funeral arrangements as the flag-draped coffin with what was their son or daughter, brother or sister, husband or wife, is on the way home. Only when buried, and we help them with the expenses here as well, do the conversations turn to additional monies and benefits. This is often pressed by the officer, as the families seldom think in terms of what might be their entitlements, and are often surprised at what they hear. In addition to the already paid death gratuity, there is the Servicemembers' Group Life Insurance (SGLI) policy payment of $250,000, some of the premiums of which are paid for by the now dead marine. If married at the time of death there are monthly stipends that come in from Social Security, the VA, and the Department of Defense, and these very frequently are more than what the deceased may have made while alive. Something to keep in mind, however, is the burden of combat deaths fall most often on the Privates First Class and Lance Corporals; whose average yearly wages are $17,000. These benefits of course depend on how many children and other specific circumstances, and decrease over time due to age or a surviving child's student status.

I have queried the Marine Corps Legislative Liaison staff members who work so closely with your own staffs on a full range of issues, about inquiries related to deaths in an attempt to gain some insights on how all of these financial arrangements are received by the families of the fallen. We really have no trends other than perhaps the issue of post-death payments from VA and Social Security that we work to expedite. Anecdotally, I can tell you that there are many spouses grieving over a death who make the point that it would be very helpful to have an increase in the SGLI option to two or even four times its current amount, with the cost of buying a home and college the most common rationale. They are not bitter, angry, or disappointed at what they receive, but in retrospect wish they had taken out more insurance.

In conclusion, on behalf of your marines and their families, I thank this committee for your continued and indispensable support during these demanding times as we attempt to defend America, and spread the freedoms we enjoy to everyone man, woman, and child in Iraq and Afghanistan. I would also add that no recruit that raises his or her hand and swears a solemn oath to serve and protect this Nation—even unto death—joins the Marine Corps for long-term financial benefit. They certainly never give a thought to programs that will assist them and their families in the event they are severely disabled or killed. It is all ultimately part of the recruiting and retention package, however, and in an increasingly difficult recruiting environment particularly for the two Services shouldering the greatest burden of death and injury in this war, we must take a very hard look at anything that will set the minds of those in the war and their families at ease. Regardless of what uniform they wear, where they serve, or what their specialty is, if they move against our enemies in this global war they need to be supported in the way they deserve. We must also not forget the disabled who have unique financial and mental health difficulties those of us who are healthy can never fathom. Their obstacles are great, their recovery forever, and we must not let them slip into the abyss that comes with being put aside and forgotten.

I again thank the committee for your unwavering support for your Marine Corps and all our great Nation's servicemembers.

Chairman WARNER. Thank you very much, General Nyland, for your personal reference to the members of this committee. We have worked hard and we will continue.

General Moseley.

STATEMENT OF GEN. T. MICHAEL MOSELEY, USAF, VICE CHIEF OF STAFF, UNITED STATES AIR FORCE

General MOSELEY. Mr. Chairman, Senator Levin, distinguished committee members, thank you for holding these hearings today and for the opportunity to address these critical issues for our folks. You, in this committee, have been stalwart stewards for the defense of our great republic, and we truly appreciate your concern and continued support for our folks.

In this global war on terrorism, our airmen, Active, Guard, Reserve, and civilians are all fighting as one cohesive team with an outstanding joint team of soldiers, sailors, marines, and coast guardsmen. This global war is not isolated to a single geographic location and includes a multitude of activities in the execution of these combat tasks, as well as the preparation for these combat duties. Today's airmen are smart, courageous, and determined. They are doing what they have been trained to do, and they do it with excellence.

It is my opinion that we can do better to address benefits and compensation for them and their families. If a servicemember is wounded in action, the Air Force will do whatever it takes to help them recover, and when a military member pays the ultimate price for his country, I believe with all my heart that we must take care of those left behind, their families, and particularly their children. We cannot lessen this pain and we cannot heal this hurt, but we can, for sure, help them with the unforgiving demands of continuing their lives without a father or without a mother.

Mr. Chairman, the Department of the Air Force is a part of a great joint team fighting a tough fight, a fight that we must win. But none of the challenges in that fight are more personal for us here at this table or more important than taking care of our troops and their families.

Again, thank you for your continued support of our soldiers, sailors, airmen, marines, and coast guardsmen. I, as well as my colleagues, look forward to your questions. Thank you, Mr. Chairman.

[The prepared statement of General Moseley follows:]

PREPARED STATEMENT BY GEN. T. MICHAEL MOSELEY, USAF

Mr. Chairman, Senator Levin, and committee members, thank you for holding these hearings today. You have been stalwart stewards for the defense of our great Republic.

In war our top priorities are to accomplish the mission and to take care of our people. Back on the home front, the best thing we can do for those fighting our wars is to take care of their families. We owe our military men and women the certainty that if they are severely injured or killed, we will look after them and their loved ones.

If a servicemember is wounded in action, the Air Force will do whatever it takes to help them recover. Our Palace Helping Airmen Recover Together (HART) program follows Air Force wounded in action until they return to Active-Duty or are medically retired. We work to retain them on Active-Duty if it is at all possible. If we are unable to return airmen to Active-Duty, we work to get them civilian employment within the Air Force. Finally, we also make sure they are counseled on all the benefits they are entitled to within the Department of Defense (DOD), Department of Veterans' Affairs (VA), and the Department of Labor. I am thankful for the work Dr. Chu has done in standing up the Joint Support Operations Center. This DOD center is a great complement to our own program and will ensure that no injured airmen is forgotten or neglected. As of today, 166 airmen have been wounded in action; 145 of them have returned to Active-Duty; 1 has medically separated; and 20 are on convalescent leave or awaiting a medical board.

At Walter Reed and at Andrews, I've met many of the injured airmen and soldiers returning from war. I am proud of them and their courage as they travel the hard road to recovery. Every airman I've met wanted to return to Active-Duty and their unit. Our skilled medical personnel have helped improve the odds of a full recovery far beyond the odds available even 10 years ago. We currently have 11 airmen being treated on an out-patient basis due to Operation Iraqi Freedom (OIF) and Operation Enduring Freedom (OEF) injuries.

What of the killed in action (KIA)? When a military member pays the ultimate price for his country, I believe with all my heart that we must take care of those they left behind—their family. We cannot lessen their pain, we cannot heal their hurt, but we can help them with the unforgiving demands of continuing their lives. Here is where the Air Force focuses on the whole experience: from compassionately making the initial contact, to gently organizing the transition period and funeral, and finally to loyally helping the family adjust to the long-term loss.

I am proud of our professional and compassionate Casualty Assistance Officers (CAOs). These highly trained volunteers are with the families from the point they are initially notified, and stick with them for as long as they are needed. This personal relationship is crucial to properly taking care of the bereaved.

The CAO, alongside chaplains and other friends within the community, help the family cope with difficult emotions, while also helping them navigate complex financial hurdles. Dr. Chu has detailed the financial assistance we currently give to the families. In 2003, this committee helped change the law; increasing the gratuity and providing it to the family of any military member, who died while on Active-Duty, and we truly appreciate the full support.

We continue to work to improve the Air Force's process and attention to detail in taking care of the airmens' families.

Besides the death gratuity and payment for funeral expenses, the other major payment to our airmen is done under the Servicemembers' Group Life Insurance (SGLI). This low cost insurance is a benefit that almost every airman uses. Currently 99 percent of all enlisted members are covered by SGLI with 88 percent electing the maximum coverage of $250,000. Only 0.02 percent elected zero coverage. Amongst the officer ranks, 92 percent elected the maximum SGLI coverage. Only 4 percent elect zero coverage. SGLI is a great benefit, and I appreciate your desire to strengthen it further.

Mr. Chairman and members of the committee, the Department of the Air Force is part of a great joint team fighting a global war on terrorism. We are challenged every day in the conduct of combat operations across the globe. None of the challenges, though, are more personal or more important than taking care of our airmen and their families. Thank you for the unwavering support you have given our Nation. Thank you for calling this hearing. I am grateful to you for the opportunity to reexamine this important issue.

Chairman WARNER. Thank you very much, General. This has been an excellent presentation by our panel.

I again mentioned, Senator McCain, that you were among those who recommended that we bring up the military services to make there is sort of a unity of views here, and I think we are achieving that.

Again, in recognition of the initiatives by Senator Sessions over a number of years on this issue, I will yield my question time to you and then take my turn at the bottom of the order. Senator Sessions.

Senator SESSIONS. Thank you, Mr. Chairman, for really giving us the first hearing. You said we were going to move on this promptly and you certainly have. I think it is time for us to bring it to a reality.

There are a lot of different ways we can do it. We will have some ideas, and I am sure the legislation that Senator Lieberman and I have offered can be improved today or in the days to come. Hopefully, we can bring it to final passage.

Dr. Chu, I would like to see us consider moving this as part of the defense supplemental, or there could be other ways it could be done. I know that is one way it would move rapidly. What are your thoughts about that?

Dr. CHU. We certainly have no objection, Senator. We endorse the principle of retroactivity back to the start of current operations in October of 2001. So if it is done in a later vehicle, the authorization bill, for example, we would still be taking care of all those concerned.

Chairman WARNER. I have talked with the Majority Leader about this, and I think he has been consulting Senator Reid. I do hope that this can be achieved, Senator.

Senator SESSIONS. Thank you, Mr. Chairman. I know you are pushing to make this a reality soon.

General Nyland, I was in Iraq 2 weeks ago and in Fallujah where I met with the Marines. What a magnificent accomplishment those marines demonstrated there. That was a tough battle. I think it is too little appreciated just how difficult it was. They had to go house to house against a determined, often suicidal enemy. We lost 70, maybe 80 marines in that tough battle. They performed with courage and fidelity to duty. They never waivered and there were never any complaints, just "we want to do the job." It was just thrilling to be with them, and I wanted to say that.

The life insurance, SGLI, applies to every service person no matter what they do and how they may lose their life. But if it is in a hostile zone, they do not have to pay the premiums on the extra $150,000, from $250,000 to $400,000. I think there is some distinction between a person in a hostile fire zone and a person not in a hostile fire zone who may lose their life. I would love to make sure we have some flexibility for you and members in uniform who have wrestled with these issues for years to reach the right decision about how to say the death benefit is paid. That is what we are really talking about. It would only affect the death benefit portion here.

Do you have thoughts about that? Would you like more flexibility and an opportunity to work on the details more carefully before this legislation finally moves?

General NYLAND. Senator, yes, sir. First, thank you for the comments on the marines, and I would be remiss if I did not add that we did that in company with my great brother and soldier, Dick Cody, and his soldiers.

Senator SESSIONS. You are correct. There were quite a number of Army personnel in that fight.

General NYLAND. I think I would like a little more time to understand the details, sir. For me, if a young man or a young lady steps forward and raises his right hand to serve this great Nation, I think we have to be very careful about making any distinctions about the type of service that they rendered. There are some additional benefits if you are in combat, obviously, with tax exclusions, hostile fire pay, and hazardous duty pay. We have to be very careful not to omit those who might be training to go, or perhaps, one who has already returned and is having trouble adapting and perhaps loses his life through a late night at the club, trying to come to grips with what he may have seen over there, and accidentally loses his life on the way home. So my concern is that if an individual wears the cloth of this great Nation, we just have to understand completely and be very careful about how we would characterize his service.

I think we have some vehicles in our line-of-duty investigations that would allow us to address that, but I do think we probably ought to make sure we really have it right before we slap the table, sir.

Senator SESSIONS. Well, I thank you for your insights into that.

Mr. Epley, the legislation that Senator Lieberman and I offered would bring SGLI up to $400,000, which I think in contemporary terms is probably a better number, or a more legitimate number, than $250,000. I noticed the Veterans' Affairs Committee is concerned with this number and has suggested maybe just going up to $300,000. But this is basically a program that is paid for by the service personnel, and they would not be required to take the upper limits, although they would get the extra hostile fire pay if they were killed in hostile fire.

What are your thoughts about that? What difficulties or problems do you see in raising the life insurance from $250,000 to $400,000?

Mr. EPLEY. Senator, we at the VA support the concept of increasing the benefit in SGLI. We have looked at some different numbers. Currently, as you indicated, the insurance program is paid for through the premiums that are paid for by the service men and women themselves, and the current rate is about 6.5 cents per $1,000 of coverage in insurance. Our estimates are that we could keep that rate if the insurance were increased up to about $300,000 per member, and if the rate were to go higher, we might have to increase the premium rates per month, per member or have it subsidized. That could be done more simply, I think, as was discussed here, through the payment that is currently called the death gratuity.

Senator SESSIONS. If there is a modest increase in rate, should they not be given an opportunity to choose to go up? How would that adversely impact the basic insurance payments?

Mr. EPLEY. Certainly they should be, and they are given the choice to choose the amount. They can choose below what is now the maximum of $250,000 and make a designation. I trust that we would continue to allow them to do that, and the premium rates would be determined by the actuarial staff to just make sure it was the fairest, most economical method for all the service men and women.

Senator SESSIONS. Just briefly, I will ask any of the Vice Chiefs here if they would like to comment on a concern that I have heard that spouses or perhaps other designated beneficiaries should be notified of any change or elimination by the servicemember of the life insurance benefit. In other words, sometimes a spouse may have a valuable insight into how much life insurance should be taken out and whether it should be stopped or not. Would that be a positive benefit for your commanders as they counsel soldiers on SGLI?

Admiral NATHMAN. Sir, I believe there should be some counseling about the benefits, obviously. I believe it is a personal choice, and the personal choice is he is electing to have a certain service level, as it were, and it is very typical of what we do in the civilian world. So I think once you provide the counseling with the benefits, then that should remain a personal decision as to the level of coverage and benefit.

Senator SESSIONS. What if the servicemember has taken out life insurance, the $250,000 under current law, and decides to just eliminate that? Should the spouse be consulted in any way or be given notice in any way of the servicemember's choice in that regard?

General NYLAND. I would submit, sir, that I think that as an individual, he or she ought to feel an obligation to inform their spouse and/or a parent, or whoever the beneficiary might be. I am not 100 percent sure how we would handle that and still let it be the individual's notification vice whether the command became involved. I think I would have to think about that a little bit more as part of the study as we go forward.

Senator SESSIONS. Well, you never know. People make decisions sometimes impulsively. Sometimes consulting with a spouse would help make a better decision and might help relieve families and children from an adverse and unwise, impetuous decision for a few bucks a month which could, in fact, jeopardize their family. I am not sure it would be too burdensome if we at least asked that there be notice given to a spouse before a policy is dropped.

General NYLAND. Yes, sir. I agree with that. We certainly encourage our members to discuss it with their family when they make those decisions. In my own mind, I am not yet sure of the exact mechanics of how we would do something like that.

Senator SESSIONS. Well, these are real-life decisions, some of the things we discussed in this legislation.

Thank you, Mr. Chairman. My time is expired.

Chairman WARNER. Thank you very much, Senator Sessions.

If I might just take a minute. Thank you, General Nyland, for acknowledging that it was a joint operation in Fallujah with the United States Army. I had a very modest role in the Marine Corps as a uniformed officer at one time years ago.

But throughout history, the Marines and the Army have fought side by side, I suppose most notably in World War I in which my father participated as an Army doctor in the trenches with the Marines who distinguished themselves at the battle of Belleau Wood. At that time, Pershing acknowledged that they might have some permanence in the military annals of our history. I believe in this operation in Iraq, Desert I as well as Desert II, the Marines and the Army have written a chapter about jointness.

At this point, Admiral Nathman, how many thousand sailors are in country in Iraq now?

Admiral NATHMAN. Well, sir, if you look at the total theater right now, depending on the battle group or the——

Chairman WARNER. Let us take in country on the ground. I mean, it is surprising the number that are on the ground.

Admiral NATHMAN. Yes, sir. We are probably around the 18,000 level right now.

Chairman WARNER. Correct, in country.

Admiral NATHMAN. Yes, sir.

Chairman WARNER. Boots on the ground.

Admiral NATHMAN. Kuwait, Bahrain, Qatar, Iraq, yes, sir. They are serving in many different ways, supporting the Army in terms of logistics support or moving cargo or medical support. There is a tremendous medical presence also because of our relationship with the Marine Corps, obviously, in terms of the type of on-scene casualty care, but also the right kind of surgical care that has done so much to make sure that our members survive some pretty horrific injuries.

Chairman WARNER. Well, it has been a joint operation. Magnificent.

How many on the ground in country in Iraq and Afghanistan with you, General Moseley?

General MOSELEY. Mr. Chairman, we have 33,000 deployed into the Central Command (CENTCOM) area of responsibility (AOR) for Afghanistan and Iraq, with about 400 aircraft.

Senator SESSIONS. Mr. Chairman, I would just note that General Sattler, the Marine commander there in Fallujah, took me first and foremost to the hospital operated by the Navy Medical Corps and bragged on them extensively. I flew in and out, as we all have, with Air Force pilots who are flying in at risk every day.

Chairman WARNER. Magnificent jointness.

Senator Levin.

Senator LEVIN. Thank you, Mr. Chairman.

I would like to ask each of you about whether or not the amount of the death gratuity should depend upon where the death takes place. Three of you have commented either very forcefully or more subtly against making that distinction. I want to ask each of you that question.

General Nyland, I do not think I have to ask you that question. I think you have basically answered it. But I gather it is your strong feeling that there should not be a distinction, or before any such distinction is made, that there should be a whole lot greater consideration given to creating that distinction. Why do you not put it in your words again?

General NYLAND. Yes, sir. I agree exactly with the latter part of your statement. I think we need to understand before we put any distinctions on the great service of these wonderful young men and women who wear the cloth of this Nation, either going forward into combat, training to go to combat, or in tsunami relief. They are all performing magnificently. I think we have to be very cautious in drawing distinctions.

Senator LEVIN. It has not been made to date, and you would not instinctively put that distinction into it.

General NYLAND. No, sir, I would not.

Senator LEVIN. Admiral.

Admiral NATHMAN. Well, sir, it is kind of where the debate started. This has often been about how we take care of the survivors, the families, and the children. They cannot make a distinction. I do not believe we should either. I think I am right where Senator Sessions was, that this is such a strong bond, this is a covenant bond with those who serve. So we should not make a distinction. We do in terms of compensation for people in combat. There is combat pay, there are those kinds of things that recognize that they are actually in that AOR in combat, but in terms of taking care of the men and women that they leave behind, there should be no distinction.

Senator LEVIN. All right. Dr. Chu, I will get back to you at the end, but General Cody.

General CODY. Sir, I agree with my comrades here. We have discussed it at length. This is a very complex world we live in right now. The amount of training we do is changing every day. We have soldiers, airmen, sailors, marines, and coast guardsmen moving all around this world. It is about service to this country, and I think we need to be very careful about making this $100,000 decision based upon what type of action. I would rather err on the side of covering all deaths rather than try to make the distinction.

Senator LEVIN. All right. Thank you.

General MOSELEY. Sir, I agree. I believe geographically we have people in advance composite force training preparing for combat, which in some cases is as lethal as actual combat. We have the mechanisms in place to work with Dr. Chu and the Department on line-of-duty assessments relative to determining were those actual line-of-duty deaths or not. So those mechanisms are in place, and we would welcome the opportunity to work with the Department to finesse those details. But I believe a death is a death, and our service men and women should be represented that way.

Senator LEVIN. Now, Dr. Chu, the proposal that you have made does make that distinction, and I am wondering if you would comment on the statements that you have heard here this morning, as to why that distinction is included in your——

Dr. CHU. I would be glad to. I think one of the things that I would emphasize, as General Moseley pointed out, is that S. 77 gives the Department latitude. It does cull out training accidents specifically in the combat-related special compensation standard that it sets.

I do think it is a question of objectives. Our premier objective here is to provide for those who have fallen in Iraq and Afghanistan—to their surviving families, as I indicated in my testimony, a total payment of $500,000.

Then I think there are a variety of other objectives that people have spoken to. One objective asks, should we recognize this service in a special way? If the objective is to provide for all families, then I think one increases the emphasis on SGLI, and perhaps picks a little different figure on what we today call the death gratuity. I think as the witnesses have indicated, this is an issue we will work with Congress on as to what are our objectives are, what we want to achieve, what our purpose is in making these various changes.

S. 77 does give the Department latitude to take a line-of-duty approach. It is well within, as I understand it, the language in the proposal.

Senator LEVIN. Is the administration's proposal in the budget going to include that distinction?

Dr. CHU. We think that the kind of approach that Senator Sessions and Senator Lieberman have taken in their draft, which gives the Department latitude to recognize the wide range of circumstances we face today and the perhaps wider range of circumstances we face tomorrow, is the right way to go. We would prefer not to enshrine specific choices in statute.

Senator LEVIN. But you are going to have to budget for those choices, are you not?

Dr. CHU. We understand that.

Senator LEVIN. So is the budget that you are going to submit going to include a distinction of that kind or not?

Dr. CHU. The immediate budgeting for this, as I understand the plan, is to include it in our supplemental funding because we have a significant retroactive payment we need to make.

Senator LEVIN. I am saying, are you going to assume the distinction as to where the death took place in your budget request.

Dr. CHU. That is not a decision that is before us. The question of what the future costs will be turns importantly on the level of hostilities. That is not a foreseeable event at this stage.

Senator LEVIN. But is the retroactive payment that is going to be in the budget going to make the distinction which we talked about?

Dr. CHU. The Department's approach on these payments will be to propose they be financed as part of the supplemental financing. Therefore, we will finance them as they occur, whatever rules are adopted on this point.

Senator LEVIN. Does that mean you have not made the decision on retroactivity?

Dr. CHU. No, sir. We support the principle of retroactivity.

Senator LEVIN. But are you going to apply retroactivity to deaths which occurred anywhere to people on Active-Duty during this period or only in the areas of Iraq and——

Dr. CHU. As I think the subject matter of this morning's hearing emphasizes, we have no authority at the moment to pay anything beyond the current level of what people call a death gratuity. We are seeking higher limits for both SGLI and the death gratuity. Whatever rules pertain to those payments, obviously, we will follow in our budgeting practices, but we support the kind of flexibility Senator Sessions has built into his bill.

Senator LEVIN. I do not think that you have answered the question, because you have to make an assumption in the budget one way or the other when it comes to retroactive deaths. So, of course, you are going to follow the law, but you are going to make a proposal relative to the budget which is going to assume one way or the other, and I do not think you have answered the question.

Dr. CHU. The larger assumption in making a budgetary forecast is what is the level of hostilities that we are going to confront, and that is unknowable, obviously, at the present time.

Senator LEVIN. Retroactivity is very knowable.

Dr. CHU. Retroactivity is a different matter, yes, sir.

Senator LEVIN. My time is up.

Chairman WARNER. You can have another question.

Senator LEVIN. Let me just ask one more, because it goes really to the same issue. You have made the same distinction, I believe, in the administration's proposal as to where the death occurred as to whether or not the premium will be paid on the life insurance. As I understand the proposal, the extra premium for the $150,000 would be paid where the person is in the area of hostility or the area of operation (AO).

Dr. CHU. I believe the language of Senator Sessions and Senator Lieberman's bill is AO.

Senator LEVIN. Right. Is that same distinction going to be in the administration's proposal relative to the life insurance premium?

Dr. CHU. We support the notion that the provision in the proposed legislation puts forward the idea that we ought to provide some degree of coverage, and what we have recommended is the change in coverage that is being advanced here this morning for a servicemember, even if he or she declines the SGLI program. That is the purpose of this feature of the package. For those who have already elected it, we would, of course, rebate or reduce their premiums accordingly.

Senator LEVIN. My final question goes to the issue of whether or not we should deduct from the SBP payment, the VA payment, and DIC payment. If we do that, we eliminate any benefit, as I understand it, for a significant portion of our service personnel from that VA benefit.

Mr. EPLEY. They are offset now.

Senator LEVIN. Then the offset means that there is no benefit from that benefit for a significant percentage of our troops. DOD's plan, is actually—if we are going to deduct the VA benefit from it, it does not leave them with any benefit from it at all.

Now, my question is this. In what percentage do we know, Dr. Chu, of the cases where we have death benefits paid, these annuity benefits, and where there is this deduction of the one from the other does that mean, in effect, there is only one annuity? Do we know what percentage?

Dr. CHU. I will need to get that number for the record for you, Senator.

Senator LEVIN. Could it be as many as half?

Dr. CHU. I do not know off the top of my head, Senator. I think this question of the offset raises much broader issues that go beyond the care of deceased servicemembers. Offsets are built into the Social Security system, both in private pension plans and public plans. As Mr. Epley testified, the DIC is paid to 212,000 survivors. That is much bigger than the casualty group in Iraq and Afghanistan. I think we are opening a much bigger window, and a much bigger debate if we want to look at the offset issue.

People who select DIC do get a benefit from it. That payment, as you have noted and others have noted this morning, is tax-free, which is not true of the SBP amounts.

Senator LEVIN. Our quick analysis is that a married servicemember who is an E–4, 23 years of age, that the spouse would get no benefit whatsoever if the SBP annuity benefit is offset by the DIC benefit.

Dr. CHU. That is likely.

Senator LEVIN. I think it is important to us that we know what these numbers are.

Dr. CHU. We would be delighted to get those numbers for you, Senator.

[The information referred to follows:]

There are about 275,000 families receiving Survivor Benefits Plans (SBP) benefits. Of these, roughly 21,000 (7.6 percent) have a reduced benefit as a result of the Dependency and Indemnity Compensation (DIC) offset. Another 25,000 (9 percent) have total offsets and receive only DIC. In all of these cases, the spouse was refunded all premiums paid for the portion of SBP no longer payable. The effect is to pay the surviving spouses of participating members first with any free coverage through DIC with an increase for any SBP above that, charging premiums only for the added amount of SBP actually payable.

Senator LEVIN. Thank you very much, Dr. Chu, and thank you for your service. I join our chairman in thanking you. Apparently you are going to be leaving at some point fairly soon, from what he says, and I want to join him in thanking you for your service to the country.

Chairman WARNER. Thank you, Senator Levin.

Senator McCain.

Senator McCAIN. Thank you, Mr. Chairman. I want to thank the administration for coming forward with this initiative. I think it is obvious that there is unanimity within Congress that we need to act on this compelling issue.

Dr. Chu, can we expect specific legislation from the DOD, or do we wait until legislation is generated here?

Dr. CHU. It is our intent, sir, with our transmission of legislative language, which follows the budget, to send our proposed——

Senator MCCAIN. A specific legislative proposal.

Dr. CHU. Yes, sir, it is our intent to do so.

Senator MCCAIN. Which I am sure the chairman will act on very quickly.

Chairman WARNER. That is with the main budget? We talked about the supplemental option here. I think Senator McCain's question is very important in terms of timing. If it is the desire of the leadership of Congress, that is, on the Senate side, to try and do the supplemental, I would urge that you consider the timing of your submission.

Dr. CHU. Thank you, sir. I appreciate that guidance.

Senator MCCAIN. Also, Dr. Chu, there are differences in the Guard and Reserve with the way they are paid and the way they handle retirement, et cetera. I would imagine the Guard and Reserves will be included in this as well in every way.

Dr. CHU. Yes, sir.

Senator MCCAIN. The nature of this conflict is different than any other—by the way, I also want to associate myself with the uniformed people's remarks here. This kind of conflict has a gray area. B–2 bombers flew from the United States to combat missions in Afghanistan. If a B–2 had crashed on landing in the United States, that is a combat mission. So I think we have to make this legislation all-encompassing, otherwise we would be in enormous gray areas which would be, first, difficult to define and, second of all, as the uniformed witnesses have testified here, all these men and women in the military are in this together, no matter where they are.

But the nature of this conflict is such that there are much larger instances of wounds that require amputations. This, obviously, is a significant disability for any American, although the recovery exhibited by many of these young men and women is remarkable. But it makes for a very difficult life in the future.

General Nyland, General Hagee briefed me on a program that the Marine Corps has, which I think is important, and I understand the other Services do not have anything quite like it. It is called the Marine for Life Program. Would you describe that for the committee? Because I think that somehow we ought to either legislatively, financially, or some other way encourage this type of program.

General NYLAND. Yes, sir. The Marine for Life is a program that we started some time ago to celebrate the honorable service of any marine returning to society. It is designed, through the use of hometown links and our inspector and instructor staffs, to help a young marine reestablish himself or herself in the civilian community through the resources of the hometown link and the people.

What we have done most recently is to expand that to a second phase that we call Injured Support Program. In this regard, we are basically trying to help these disabled marines not only with resettlement into society but also to get through all the bureaucracy and red tape that allows them to get their ready-to-go. So this entails——

Senator MCCAIN. Tell us how it works, General.

General NYLAND. Yes, sir. We are putting a staff officer over at the VA. We will work individually with our marines, in essence, in individual case management, to take them through the medical evaluation and the performance evaluation boards, so that we link them quickly with the VA so there is no break in the pay between the Defense Finance and Accounting Service (DFAS) pay system and the VA pay system. In essence, we assist the marine with that transition until he or she is back where he or she wants to be, a useful member of society.

Senator MCCAIN. Someone who has suffered the loss of a limb has some difficulty in their readjustment and acquiring sufficient vocational skills. Do you believe that this legislation addresses that problem sufficiently? I will begin with you, General Nyland, and ask the other witnesses.

General NYLAND. Sir, I actually believe that is beyond the scope of this particular legislation, but I certainly share your concern because these are magnificent young men and women. As you have pointed out, in many cases their recoveries are remarkable, some to include returning to Active-Duty and combat again. It is a life-changing event, and the education is an area that I think we have to look very closely at as we look at this package of benefits that goes to the disabled veterans, as well as those who regrettably lose their lives.

Senator MCCAIN. I go to you next, General Cody.

General CODY. Yes, sir. We have a program very similar to the Marines and call ours DS3 that we stood up in recognition of the wounds you are talking about, Senator. Armor that we are providing our soldiers and marines today in ground combat is saving lives, but we have a significant number of amputees and other serious injuries. To date, we have about 271 Active Guard and Reserve soldiers that are in the DS3 program, some double amputees, and we are working very closely with the VA on working the transition and benefits.

But DS3 is a 5- to 10-year commitment by the Army to each one of these soldiers and their families to not only take care of their health care, but also their financial care. It starts when the soldier arrives at Landstuhl, coming out of theater. We have a cell there. We have a cell at Brooke, as well as Walter Reed, and we have just hired on about 54 case workers to handle each one of these individual soldiers, plus their family members.

I also agree with General Nyland. It is outside the scope of what we are talking about today, but it is something that we have to come back and look at.

We are looking at our regulations. We have several soldiers right now that are amputees that we put back on Active-Duty. One sergeant, in particular, lost his right leg above the knee and is serving now as a master sergeant. He is a combat medic. His name is Sergeant Luis Rodriguez. He lost it in Mosul. He is still on Active-Duty, and he is now a combat medic trainer there at Fort Campbell, Kentucky. We are looking at our regulations, because there are certainly technical advances in the prothesis devices that we are providing our servicemembers.

We also are looking at other things. We have also teamed the Helping Our Heroes Foundation with our DS3 program, which is a separate foundation that teams with industry. For those that we do transition or they elect to transition out of the military, our case workers will follow and team them up with some of our larger corporations who have stepped forward that are teaming with VA and getting educational benefits and help in the family transition.

There is more we can do. Like I say, we are dealing with about 271 cases right now. We have had over 7,200 wounded during this fight, and we are looking at each case individually and making sure that we are doing it. But I think it is outside the scope right now of what we are dealing with here, but it is something that probably deserves a better look.

General MOSELEY. Senator, thanks for that question.

We are attempting to poach as many good ideas as we can from the Marine Corps program, which is outstanding. We have a program. We have had 166 airmen severely injured. We have had 145 return to Active-Duty as amputees. We have 20 right now awaiting medical evaluation boards, and we think 16 of them will be returned to Active-Duty. Of the 166 wounded, we have only had one that we have had to discharge and that was a double amputee that actually wanted to go to school.

Of the 145, we have amputees back on Active-Duty, to include some of our special operations guys who have been responsible for working with the Army on reducing the load of the packs, bettering the com gear, et cetera.

When we have a wounded airman, we have a casualty assistance representative from U.S. Air Forces, Europe (USAFE) that meets with that person at Landstuhl and stays with that person when we get them back to Walter Reed, Bethesda, or Malcolm Grove. Then we have a person permanently assigned to that injured airman that stays with him through the next set of processes, to include the medical evaluation board.

Senator, we are partnering with the VA, but I can tell you where we can do better. When a person separates and goes to a small community, there are certainly less opportunities in a small community for continued care. We are beginning to look at opportunities to partner with the other services to see if there is not something that we can pool better, whether it is Veterans of Foreign Wars (VFW) or whether it is some agencies out there in smaller communities to make this better for our folks. That is the piece where we think we can do better. We do not have an answer for you yet, but we are working on that.

Admiral NATHMAN. Senator McCain, we do have continuing care for our sailors. In fact, what I think is interesting is the continuing care that we are talking about includes the Marine Corps. We get the Marine Corps' severely injured ready for that decision about Marine for Life, as they transition into civilian life. We have a very interesting and good relationship with the Army at Walter Reed because they are particularly good at prothesis care and transitioning those severely injured marines and sailors into the right type of prosthetic device that allows them to do what they need to do.

But to answer your question directly, I do not believe this legislation covers that matter, but the question is certainly a very good one about how we want to go look at this to make sure we are doing the right thing by our people. Does it imply the right type of relationship with our organizations like American Legion or VFW and imply a different relationship with the VA? I believe your question means that we ought to scrutinize this and look for the opportunities to do the right thing by our severely injured sailors and marines that transition to civilian life.

Our goal has been to try and return our severely injured back to Active-Duty. One of the questions that is implied in that, is what are we doing to make sure that we are stimulating those young men and women to do that besides just taking care of their attendant physical needs.

Thank you, sir.

Senator MCCAIN. Thank you. Mr. Chairman, we probably have to look at this more in the future, but from my conversations, it is one of the biggest issues that many of these young men and women face.

By the way, I think it is noteworthy that $10 million is being expended on an amputee rehabilitation facility out at Walter Reed. It may be a little overdue, but the fact is I do not think we ever anticipated this element in war. I believe that people should be assured that whatever is necessary, we will fund to care for these people.

I thank you, Mr. Chairman.

Chairman WARNER. I thank you for bringing that up, Senator McCain. I have the privilege of joining with Secretary Wolfowitz today at the designation of the military severely injured joint support operations center, a new concept that is being set up. I appreciate you bringing that important subject to the attention of the members here at this hearing this morning. Thank you.

Mr. Nelson has departed I see. Then, Mr. Dayton, I believe you are next.

Senator DAYTON. Thank you, Mr. Chairman.

I want to commend my colleagues who have sponsored this important legislation, and I am proud to be a cosponsor of a couple of those initiatives.

I want to associate myself with the comments of the distinguished ranking member, Senator Levin, about this coverage including all servicemembers serving in all locations and whose deaths occur under all circumstances. I agree with what he said, that someone who is killed in a training exercise—and I have had that experience with a couple of Minnesotans since I joined the Senate and served on this committee—their losses are just as immense as those families who lost servicemembers in combat areas. So I do not think it is appropriate to distinguish one type of death from another.

Dr. Chu, your testimony about the various kinds of coverage is very helpful. I do not mean to quibble here, but if servicemembers are carrying their own life insurance through a group policy, if they are paying what you say are modest premiums, to the extent that that is not subsidized by the Government, I would question whether that can be fairly termed a Government-provided benefit. Anybody can do that, and probably should do that, in almost any occupation, especially if they have a family, anywhere in this society. If they are paying their own premiums, for the Government to claim that as a benefit seems to me inflates this number quite dramatically. It would be appropriate, to the extent that it is being subsidized, but not to the extent that the individual is paying that cost himself or herself.

Dr. CHU. It is, as you are aware, Senator, subsidized. The Department picks up all risks beyond normal peacetime risks, war risks especially, and as you point out, training risks are important in that regard. So someone who was a flyer could not buy this insurance at this rate commercially.

Senator DAYTON. What percent of the premium for somebody serving in a combat area is paid by the individual?

Dr. CHU. We basically pay all the combat deaths.

Senator DAYTON. I am sorry?

Dr. CHU. We basically pay all the combat deaths. It does not work quite that way mechanically, but that is the practical import.

Senator DAYTON. When you talk about the administration's proposal at the end here that would increase the coverage to $400,000, that additional $150,000 insurance would be funded by the Government when the member is serving in an AO designated by the Secretary of Defense?

Dr. CHU. That is correct.

Senator DAYTON. Again, you would pay that. But if the individual under this proposal were serving in a noncombat zone and was killed while in service, that would not apply?

Dr. CHU. They would still be eligible for the $400,000. I think that is the important point that we are trying to emphasize here. We need, as Senator Sessions' and Senator Lieberman's bill does, to raise SGLI's number. It has not been addressed for a while. We need to provide the surviving families, as you suggest, regardless of circumstance, with a larger bequest so they can deal with their issues in a cohesive way. So we would like to get SGLI increased. I think that is the first big point I would like to emphasize this morning.

Second, we would like to make the increment something the Government pays for in an AO designated by the Secretary. That is intended specifically to deal with combat areas. It is also intended to deal with individuals who—they are small in number—but a few do decline. Then as Senator Sessions' questions suggest about should the spouses be consulted, there is substantial regret ex post. So we are trying to begin to create a little bit of a different construct here with this package. I think his bill has exactly that feature in it, if I recall it correctly. We celebrate that.

Senator DAYTON. Especially, again, people with families, the cost factor, depending again how much the individual is paying and how much the military is paying——

Dr. CHU. The charge for that $250,000 I believe is $16.25 a month, and I think most people view that as a bargain.

Senator DAYTON. You mentioned also the ability to remain in military housing for 6 months. Is that the same housing that the family is in presently on base?

Dr. CHU. Yes, sir.

Senator DAYTON. Okay, so they have that option. Do you think 6 months is sufficient time? I have heard concerns expressed by a couple of surviving spouses whose children are in school. This is their support system. These are their friends, the other spouses, their children's friends. Is 6 months sufficient time?

Dr. CHU. The Government's benefit actually is more generous than just the military housing. We either allow them to stay in their housing, if that is their choice, or if they are already receiving or prefer to receive their housing allowance, we do that for 6 months. So this is, I think, a very sound package. It provides a good transition for them. My understanding is the Services manage this with extraordinary compassion.

General CODY. If I might add, Senator.

Senator DAYTON. Yes, sir.

General CODY. I have commanded a post, and we had this situation arise several times. The way the policy and regulation are written, the post commander has the authority to extend in those types of cases, and so it is not open-ended, but he has the ability to deal with the family's situation because none of them are all the same. I have never heard of one who did not extend it.

Senator DAYTON. Is that true in all Service branches?

General NYLAND. Yes.

General MOSELEY. Yes.

Senator DAYTON. I think that's appropriate.

Chairman WARNER. Senator Dayton, that is a very important question. I want the record to reflect the acknowledgement of each of the Vice Chiefs to your question as to whether or not there is uniformity in that policy. So if you would just ask each individual.

Senator DAYTON. Could I ask each of you then to respond for the record please?

General MOSELEY. It is the same in the Air Force, sir.

Senator DAYTON. Thank you.

Admiral NATHMAN. I would like to make sure of my facts, sir, but yes, sir.

Senator DAYTON. Thank you.

General NYLAND. I believe that is also the case for the Marine Corps, sir.

Senator DAYTON. All right. Thank you.

I believe I have visited with all the Minnesota families who have lost servicemembers, and generally speaking, I would say their comments support what you said in your testimony about the quality of the notification. I will—and I would be remiss if I did not, because I just met with this family just a couple weeks ago, whose son was serving in the Marine Corps and was visited by a couple of service men, but not accompanied by a chaplain. The mother was distraught because she asked if the body had been anointed, and the servicemembers did not know what that meant. Again, I am not trying to—in my position 99 percent of the things go well, and I hear about 1 percent, and I usually get it in a public setting, so I cringe. But I would be remiss if I did not take the opportunity just to ask you to review that policy and make sure that there are chaplains involved and that those who are doing this very difficult work are trained and trained not only with a manual, but in grief counseling because I think this is hugely important and it makes a huge impact. It is irreversible if it is not handled properly.

General NYLAND. Yes, sir. I certainly share your concern. I am unaware of that, but I will certainly look into that because we want this to be done properly for the families.

Senator DAYTON. I can give you the names of the family if you want to check it out.

General NYLAND. Yes, sir.

Senator DAYTON. But again, I think it is an aberration in the Marines and the Army. I have heard uniformly from the families real gratitude at the proper notification, and the support they received. But I do want to put it on the record. Thank you.

Thank you, Mr. Chairman.

Chairman WARNER. Thank you very much, Senator.

Senator Collins.

Senator COLLINS. Thank you, Mr. Chairman.

First, let me start by thanking you for scheduling this hearing so early in the session. I think that demonstrates your commitment to moving this important legislation.

I also want to congratulate my colleagues, particularly Senator Sessions, Senator Allen, Senator Lieberman, and Senator Nelson, for their leadership on this important issue.

As the chairman is well aware, I have long supported an increase in the payment that is made to the families of those who have made the ultimate sacrifice for our country. During the last Congress, I was, in fact, the chief Senate sponsor of legislation to double the death gratuity and to make it tax-free. That was, however, only a very modest first step and an inadequate one. I am very pleased to see the growing consensus that we should enact significant legislation in this regard. It is terrific to hear the administration's support for doing that promptly, as well.

Dr. Chu, there have been disturbing reports of confusion among some military personnel regarding the amount of their insurance benefits and even more troubling reports of unscrupulous financial salesmen and women having access to our military bases and peddling very expensive and often unneeded insurance products to our troops. This is very troubling because the insurance program that is already available to them is a very good one and a relatively inexpensive one, and the passage of Senator Sessions' bill will make it an even better program.

What efforts are being undertaken to inform our troops of the benefits of the insurance programs and to give them guidance so that they can make informed choices regarding their insurance purchases? Obviously, if they feel they need additional insurance, they have every right to purchase it, but this is troubling if they are being talked into buying superfluous or very expensive insurance products that they really do not need.

My second and related question is, when the legislation is enacted, as I believe it will be, to improve the insurance benefits, how will the DOD act to quickly inform our troops of the new benefits?

Dr. CHU. Ma'am, as I think you are aware, over 2 years ago, we launched in the Department for this reason and other reasons, what we call a financial readiness campaign, that basically is an effort to ensure that our people, for whom often this is their first posting, so to speak, after school, about how to manage their finances broadly, including the insurance issue.

We have been working for almost 2 years to change the Department's regulations in terms of the unscrupulous salesman issue, as you correctly point out. Unfortunately, we are under an injunction that is part of the last appropriations act that does not allow us to move forward with that directive until after the GAO renders its report, which is not expected until June 2005. If I could plead for one thing in this domain that you properly raised, if indeed our action is the vehicle for change, perhaps we could get that prohibition against action removed so we can start to deal more effectively with the unscrupulous actor.

Senator COLLINS. So the administration would support doing away with that rider. Is that correct?

Dr. CHU. Yes, ma'am.

Senator COLLINS. That limits your ability to deal with this problem.

Dr. CHU. Under present law, we cannot deal with this until after the GAO renders its report.

Senator COLLINS. But surely you could undertake efforts to make sure that the troops are better informed and have increased financial awareness. I understand that the injunction limits your ability to perhaps cut off access to the troops, but in many ways, this is an educational issue. It is a financial sophistication or awareness campaign that is needed.

Dr. CHU. We agree with you completely and that is why 2 years ago, we launched the financial readiness campaign. We can do a great deal. We are doing a great deal. I think individual base commanders are improving their policies. I particularly praise the approach that the Fort Benning commander has taken in this regard. Yes, ma'am, we can do a lot to educate people on our own without a change in the statute, but we would appreciate a revocation of the rider.

Senator COLLINS. General Cody, do you have anything you would like to add to this?

General CODY. Yes. I think, first off, I agree with Dr. Chu that we need to do more. Having commanded a large post, I can tell you that every time, when a soldier enlists, when they go to the training base, whatever training base they go to, they get financial guidance. Now, these are young soldiers, and it takes a lot of discussion about why you need insurance. Some of them do not want to buy insurance for their car, and so we have to work through all that. Of course, we have regulations that you cannot register your car on post unless you get insurance, and so each post has that and we are working it hard.

At each one of our posts, camps, and stations, soldiers, after they come out of their training base, have a 7- to 10-day transition period before they go to their units, and they have financial management classes at Fort Campbell that I am familiar with in which we give them the SGLI briefing. It is not just a 1-hour briefing. It is a whole discussion about what it means, especially if you are married. We give them the same type of briefing to watch out for people that bird dog you, quite frankly, for insurance, and other characters are out there trying to do that. They also get classes on how to buy cars. It is a full financial management program that we have been doing so that they fully understand what they need to. I think it is not where it should be, but it is certainly much better than when I joined several years ago.

Senator COLLINS. Thank you.

Mr. Chairman, I hope, as we mark up this legislation, that we will take a look at that issue as well. Again, I commend you for moving so quickly on this important issue.

Chairman WARNER. I would ask, Senator, that you and other Senators that you know of that have a particular interest in this unscrupulous situation—and that is not to cast aspersions against a lot of, I think, perfectly bona fide individuals who come on board base and work, but there is an element that we should address. Could you give me your best advice as to how we should handle this?

Senator COLLINS. I would be happy to, Mr. Chairman.

Chairman WARNER. I thank you very much.

Senator COLLINS. I spent 5 years in State government overseeing the insurance regulations. So I would be happy to assist in this area.

Chairman WARNER. So you have a background in this. Thank you very much, Senator Collins.

[The prepared statement of Senator Collins follows:]

PREPARED STATEMENT BY SENATOR SUSAN M. COLLINS

Mr. Chairman, I would like to thank you for scheduling this session on this topic so early in the session.

I have long supported an increase in the payment made to the family of those who have lost their lives in service to our country. During the 108th Congress, I was proud to be the Senate sponsor of legislation to double the death gratuity to $12,000 and make it tax free, a modest first step. I would like to reiterate my support for the measures before us today. Like all Americans, I have been greatly saddened by the loss of life in recent days during our operations in Iraq, and I commend my colleagues from both sides of the aisle for working together to again increase this benefit in this Congress, as well.

As illustrated this past weekend during the elections in Iraq, our military forces continue their noble dedication to advancing freedom and democracy even in the most difficult circumstances. The successful and truly historic elections in Iraq are a credit to their dedication and professionalism.

The young men and women of our military represent the very best our Nation has to offer. They do not join the military for monetary gain nor to have a comfortable lifestyle. They serve our Nation out of a sense of patriotism that should make each and every American proud. The patience and dedication they have shown during the months leading up to and through the election process are testament to the strength of character that is the core of our military values. In many cases, we ask our own troops to take additional risks in order to avoid injuring or killing innocent civilians. That they do this without question or regret speaks well not only of our military, but of our country.

When we send a young man or woman into harm's way, our Nation has in return a sacred obligation to them and to their families. We must ensure they go forth with the complete confidence, should the worst happen and they are called upon to make the ultimate sacrifice, that their country will care for their families and honor their service.

The death gratuity is a small token, but it assists the grieving families with their immediate financial needs. There are a variety of other programs that provide for longer-term support, but in the initial hours and days after a family has endured such a terrible loss, these funds help to alleviate monetary concerns. This benefit is commonly provided within 72 hours to the family of the servicemember who is killed while on Active-Duty.

Brigadier General John Libby, the Adjutant General of the Maine National Guard, recently wrote to me in support of this legislative initiative. More than 65 percent of Maine's Army National Guard force structure has now been mobilized and deployed in support of the global war on terrorism. Brigadier General Libby wrote, "Behind every dedicated servicemember is a dedicated service family who deserves to be taken care of in the event of the loss of their servicemember. The level of the current benefit package is not sufficient but this corrective action will honor those who serve us on a daily basis."

We can never fully repay the debt of our proud Nation to those who have laid down their lives. The best we can do is honor their memory, ensure that their sacrifice is not in vain, and help provide for their families. We must continue to assure our brave young men and women that their Nation is grateful for their service. I look forward to hearing your testimony and to working with my colleagues to ensure that we move forward to ensure that the families of those brave service men and women who give their lives for our country are properly cared for.

Thank you.

Chairman WARNER. Senator Lieberman, thank you for your patience.

Senator LIEBERMAN. Thank you, Mr. Chairman. It has been a very helpful hearing. I want to go back to the line of questioning that Senator McCain opened up about those wounded in action (WIA) because I do think, thanks to the administration announcement today, that we have a real strong consensus on the need for and, in fact, how to better care for the survivors of those killed in action (KIA). We have some details to work out, but we are going to do it, and it is clear we are going to do it with a real sense of urgency, and that is absolutely right.

I think it is appropriate to focus on those WIA. We know that we are operating in a circumstance in which the rate of survival for injury is much higher in the conflicts we are involved in now because of the extraordinary advances in medical science and technology and, to the great credit of the Pentagon and the Services, the extent to which the Services have embraced and implemented all those advances in medicine and medical technology. So it means we have people, thankfully, who are surviving but with very serious injuries and disabilities. I think we have to make sure we are doing our best for them.

It leads me to ask, just as a question of information for myself, if not for other members of the committee, because some of them are clearly not—I want to stop here. I know I have admiration but I am in awe of the numbers of those injured who remain on Active-Duty. It is nothing short of inspirational. But they are going to come to a moment where they are going to leave the Service. They go back to civilian life. Some of them are going to have impaired earning capacity because of the injury they suffered while serving on our behalf.

What do we do for them or their families? We are focused on survivors. Now, these are, fortunately, not survivors. These are the families. They are dependents. What do we do for them economically when they come out with an income-impairing disability for medical service? I leave it to whomever wants to respond.

Dr. CHU. I think I would let Mr. Epley answer that because that really is a keystone of the VA's program.

Mr. EPLEY. Yes, sir. Senator, we do have programs that are intended to address the income loss. The most significant of those programs is our disability compensation program which will pay to the veteran, based on the degree of disability, from 10 percent, which is $108 a month, up to a 100 percent benefit, which is about $2,290 per month, and additional amounts for their dependents.

Senator LIEBERMAN. What is it based on? Their service salary compensation or is it a set amount?

Mr. EPLEY. No, sir. It is based on the degree of their disability. We do a formal medical evaluation of their disability and assess it, and based on our evaluation, be they 100 percent or 50 percent disabled, we set the pay rate. You set the pay rate in law, sir.

Senator LIEBERMAN. So if there is a change, it is up to us. What I am saying is, it is a percent of what? In other words, in a lot of circumstances, clearly if somebody is injured in an accident, as a matter of court procedure, the award is based on the potential earning capacity of that person prior to the accident.

Mr. EPLEY. It is similar in the VA, sir. We have a rating schedule of disabilities, which is codified in title 38 of the U.S. Code, and it describes all of the various body systems and the disability evaluation criteria that will be used for each disability suffered by a serviceman. That is how we set the level of disability and the level of payment to be given.

May I add one more thing? You asked about if they have earning incapacitation. We do have a vocational rehabilitation program as well at VA. It is geared specifically to help those men and women who come back from service who have a disability that might affect their earning capacity. We case-manage those men and women. We try to work with the military departments to identify them, as soon as they are separating, and offer them means to determine not only what their desires are in future earnings, but also what their aptitudes are and try to engineer a program to bring back their earning capacity where it would be. We rehabilitate a little over 10,000 veterans a year through that program.

Senator LIEBERMAN. That is very reassuring. I think we ought to, Mr. Chairman, stay on top of that. I invite you—I am sure all the committee would—to come to us if you think we are not fulfilling our responsibility to those who are severely disabled as a result of service.

I want to ask another question about this. Periodically, as I am sure you know as well or better than we, there is a flurry in the media that we are not providing enough benefits to the WIA when they are in, for instance, Walter Reed. There was a flurry. We got calls a while back that we were not paying for their phone calls, at one point that the WIA had to pay for their meals. I wonder, General Cody, since we have you here if you would help clarify some of that for us.

General CODY. As I stated earlier, Senator—and I appreciate the opportunity to discuss this. This is all part of taking care of not just the soldier's wounds, but the financial care that we need to provide immediately to the family of that soldier because they have to travel, and in many cases, some of them work. Some have to pay for child care and everything else. So we are picking all that up, as soon as we can get with it, and fully understand, because each case is entirely different. We have the Mologne House. We have the Fisher House.

We have quickly reacted to this, since Operation Enduring Freedom (OEF) and Operation Iraqi Freedom (OIF), and we keep learning the different permutations of challenges that each individual family has so we can compensate for them. I think we are really doing a much better job than we have in the past on this. Each time we see some of these issues, we work through them.

Senator LIEBERMAN. Are we taking care of their phone calls, for instance, and the meals?

General CODY. Yes, sir. We are taking care of their phone calls. In fact, we are even, in most cases, not stopping the compensation they had when they left Iraq for the first 90 days, and we are doing that across the board. We are also working with DFAS, which is very complex. We are working directly with that so that the soldier or the family does not have to deal with it. We have a case worker dealing with it to ensure that the computer does not automatically start deducting. We have had those problems where all of a sudden the computer picks up the fact that they are no longer in Iraq, but oh, by the way, we paid you for 6 months and automatically started deducting. We have had several cases of that early on. So now we are putting the case worker in the loop, to take care of it.

One of the other things we are doing, as I said earlier, is teaming with Helping Our Heroes Foundation, which is a separate foundation that provides all the other benefits that we cannot do right now because of statute.

Senator LIEBERMAN. Thank you. That is very reassuring.

Mr. Chairman, my time is up. I just want to add something I was just thinking as we were talking about the financial benefits we want to provide to the survivors. There is sort of an emotional benefit as well. I have had the experience very often talking to survivors of soldiers, particularly from Connecticut, who have been killed in action where they will say please see this through to a successful conclusion in Iraq so that I will never believe that my son or daughter or husband or wife died in vain. I just saw a soldier from Walter Reed, I believe, on the TV the other night, who had lost a limb, saying watching the Iraqis vote on Sunday made him feel that what he had done had not been in vain. It was very moving. It is another kind of benefit that we can provide by sticking together until this is successfully concluded.

General MOSELEY. Senator Lieberman, can I follow up with another piece of this?

Senator LIEBERMAN. Please.

General MOSELEY. Our experience in dealing with our kids that are at Walter Reed and Bethesda is as much a family issue as it is anything. Dick and the rest of us do the same things. We get up to three family members. We fly them to the location, in this case Walter Reed for us, and we cover those expenses for 30 days. We can waiver that beyond 30 days. We have a special care provider assigned to that member and that family to ensure that those things that you are talking about do not happen. Whether they are in the Fisher House or whether they are in some other sets of quarters, we are with that family and that member every day. So we cover three family members flown at our expense, and up to 30 days. You can extend that as necessary.

Senator LIEBERMAN. It is very reassuring. Thank you all very much.

Chairman WARNER. Thank you, Senator Lieberman, for early on getting out on this basic legislation we are addressing today.

Thank you for bringing up in this colloquy the questions of family participation. All of us, I think, have been to Walter Reed, Bethesda, and other military hospitals. I remember, Senator Clinton, you and I joined way early in your first stop as a member of the Armed Services Committee, and we went together.

I also would like to have the record reflect that in last year's bill this committee put in an encouragement, based on our visitations at the hospital, including a reference to the many times that all of us have experienced the wounded saying, Senator, what can you do so that I can stay in the military even though I have lost an arm or a limb or other injury. But these old gray hairs indicate I have sort of reached back a little bit in this system, and I cannot recall a period in history where I have seen the returning soldiers more anxious to remain in the military. It is a tremendous sense of pride for their families and themselves.

General, you perhaps have the largest group. What has been your experience as a consequence of the legislation we put in last year on this?

General CODY. It has been very helpful not only in execution but in tone and tenor. It sends the right message. You are right. The first thing these soldiers, airmen, marines, and sailors that get WIA want to do is get back to their unit. There is a tremendous bond of a band of brothers and sisters. Over time, our experience shows that many want to stay, and then, many come to the conclusion that they want to move on to other things. But knowing upfront that there is that window and that possibility, our doctors say it really helps them initially during their rehabilitation, that there is no finality, no "I cannot go back to this way of life." So I think it has been extremely helpful.

As I have told you, we have put several of our noncommissioned officers (NCOs) and officers back to Active-Duty already. One captain is going back into combat. He lost his right limb. You visited him from the 3rd Armored Cavalry Regiment, Dave Rozelle. The first thing he said to me, as well as to other people, when we saw him up there after the first fight, was "I want to stay in the Army." I am proud to report to you in about a month and a half, he will deploy with the 3rd Armored Cavalry Regiment again as the commander of headquarters and Headquarters Troop.

Chairman WARNER. Without the benefit of one arm. Is that correct?

General CODY. This is the one with the missing right leg, sir.

Chairman WARNER. Oh, leg.

General CODY. Yes, sir. He also ran in a marathon. So it speaks to what this country can provide, in terms of medical care and everything else.

I firmly believe it has been very helpful. I know all of our Services are looking at our medical evaluation board procedures and our physical evaluation board procedures because those things were written in the 1970s and 1980s and, quite frankly, they do not deal with the great medical care that this country can provide. So we are looking at each case individually. I know we are all committed to not let them leave Service until we know they are making the right decision, that we have given them everything, and then we work the transitions. So I feel very positive about it.

General NYLAND. Sir, if I might add, I certainly share that. We have already one marine who lost an ankle and a foot in Afghanistan who is on duty in Iraq, and they are marvelous, marvelous young people. The advances in the prosthetics, for those who want to stay and can contribute can stay, due to the committee's action. It absolutely makes a difference.

Chairman WARNER. This committee stands by to receive any legislative proposals, Dr. Chu, to greater enhance that opportunity for these marvelous young people.

Dr. CHU. We appreciate that, sir.

Chairman WARNER. I take note of the fact that maybe some of our procedures are slightly outdated. I hope before you leave, you would take that on as one of your highest priorities, because you draw on a long experience in working in the DOD.

Dr. CHU. Thank you, sir.

Chairman WARNER. That might be one of your hallmark achievements to make sure that record is right up to date.

General MOSELEY. Mr. Chairman, can I add one more piece to that?

Chairman WARNER. Yes, of course.

General MOSELEY. Dr. Chu has been a big partner in helping us with this. Every single kid that we have talked to, his first question is, I want to stay in the Air Force. Do not throw me out. The second one is, I want to get back to my unit, the same as my other brothers here. What we have also done is if we cannot keep a person on Active-Duty, we will guarantee them a job in the civilian sector in the Air Force. We have not had to do that yet because we have 145 of them back on Active-Duty. But our counselors make it very clear to them, that if we cannot get them back to Active-Duty and if not back to that particular unit, then we will give them a job in the civilian sector of the Air Force. We have only had the one person that was medically disqualified by a medical evaluation board, and that kid is at Texas A&M University right now going to school.

Chairman WARNER. I think this chapter in history also reflects the magnificence of the people across this country. Even though they may not have family members involved, the support the American people are giving individually and collectively to the men and women of the Armed Forces. For those of us who had responsibilities during the Vietnam era, what a stark contrast to today in the manner in which those brave individuals returned home from Vietnam and had to face certain hostilities which were not of their making.

Senator Inhofe.

Senator INHOFE. Thank you, Mr. Chairman. I am glad we got into the discussion of the hospitals and of the attitudes of the kids that are there. Senator Thune and I will be going to Iraq at the end of this week, and we are going to be stopping by Landstuhl.

In fact, I have recommended that anyone going over there should make that stop.

I remember so well, Admiral, my stop there. It must have been, I guess, a couple of years ago. There was a young black lady. She was very small in stature. You will probably remember this. She got her leg caught in a fueling line and it took her down. It should have killed her, the impact was incredible. But they were trying to get her back. She could not talk except between gasps, and all she talked about was getting back to her ship. You hear this over and over and over again.

Senator Thune and I will be stopping by Landstuhl to bring this message back home. I think it is so important that we do this because I have often said we have a very unfriendly press that does not tell us accurately what is going on there.

I might add, General Cody, when we go over—we had this discussion on these hydration packs—we are taking a bunch of those back to distribute when we are there.

General CODY. Yes, sir.

Senator INHOFE. I was one of the original cosponsors of this legislation. I am very supportive of it. We have talked about this, and I have my own ideas about when you should raise the core benefits. Yet there are those, even under the passage of this bill—well, actually depending what provisions are accepted that are going to say whether or not individuals are going to be able to get an enhanced death benefit, a lot of it is tied to the idea of whether or not they reject the insurance. I am talking about out-of-combat zones. The rejection of that has to be done and signed by the troops. We talked about this earlier. What about the beneficiaries? What about the wives?

It is not unprecedented that they sign. Under the retirement benefit plan, wives have to sign, the same as the individual. I have some fairly strong feelings that we ought to comply with that and make that a part of this bill.

I will not ask each one to respond to that, but if there is anything you want to offer concerning that, do so.

Dr. CHU. Senator, if I may, I just want to reinforce the point you made. This is not a new idea. It is a central feature of the SBP as it currently exists, that the survivors need to be consulted in this decision because ultimately it affects them.

Senator INHOFE. By consulting with the spouses on the decision—what evidence is there that they have been consulted with?

Dr. CHU. In the SBP case, they have to actually sign saying they understand what the military person has chosen.

Senator INHOFE. On the life insurance.

Dr. CHU. No, on the survivor benefit plan. We have no such provision today on the life insurance.

Senator INHOFE. Okay. That is what I am referring to.

Dr. CHU. If I may, I think you and Senator Sessions and Senator Lieberman have opened an important issue with the provision in your proposed legislation that would require a mechanism by which the survivors are consulted.

Senator INHOFE. Well, I think the main thing I wanted to bring out is it is not unprecedented because we do it in retirement plans. I will not ask the rest of you to respond to that.

Senator McCain brought up a couple of things that were answered for me. I think the whole idea of amputations show as a testament to the effectiveness of the body armor. I know you have thought about this in your own mind. Of those who have suffered amputations, how many would be alive today if it had not been for that. I would suggest probably not very many.

There is always a propensity, when you are talking to elected officials, to spend more and more and more and more. I heard something on the radio this morning. Someone was saying, "Well, why is it not the same amount as the families that were victims of September 11." You can argue that it should be. But there has to be some kind of a line drawn. I would suggest to my colleagues that I think we are strapped in our military in terms of modernization, and end strength, and I do not think we are spending enough, and I have said that many times. The more you increase these benefits, most of that comes out of DOD. I think we have to keep that in mind.

Now, General Cody, you may remember the case of Fern Holland. Does that sound familiar to you? Maybe not. She was a 33-year-old Oklahoma attorney who was a civilian employee of the Army, and she was murdered, along with another American, Robert Zangus, in Iraq last March when their vehicle was ambushed by gunmen. According to DOD, this young woman was a Department of the Army civilian who was supporting OIF and assigned to the Coalition Provisional Authority (CPA).

Fern's sister contacted me recently and was concerned why there was not some kind of a benefit. You could argue this. I think that we have a tendency to open Pandora's box. There has to be a place where you stop. So if you have civilian employees that are actually in AORs in combat, that has to be addressed. But then if that is addressed, then you are going to have contract employees, even though they probably have their own benefit plans from their companies and others.

What I would like to do is ask each one of you if you have a response as to if we are going the right distance in the way it is proposed by both the administration and by the Sessions legislation. General Nyland.

General NYLAND. Yes, sir. I think it is clearly going in the right direction. I think, as Dr. Chu articulated, the $500,000 benefit or bequest, if you will, however that is ultimately packaged, has parts that I think are obviously far superior to what any of the survivors' families would receive today. I think it is an appropriate step in the right direction.

Admiral NATHMAN. Yes, sir. To your point, I understand the demarcation or distinction here is an important part of the debate we ought to have.

Senator INHOFE. Yes, it is.

General CODY. Senator, I agree. I think we are going in the right area. I am now familiar with Ms. Holland. It is something in which we have to go back and really take a look at because in this post-major combat phase of this war, we have put an awful lot of our Department of the Army civilians, as well as other Department civilians, over there as part of our reset forward in Balad and other places. They have different packages, and I think it is worthwhile for us to go back and absolutely take a good, hard look and make sure we are compensating them also.

Senator INHOFE. Sure.

General MOSELEY. Yes, sir. We are going in the right direction.

Senator INHOFE. Thank you, Mr. Chairman. I know my time is expired. I would only like to echo what everyone else has said about your duty and how much we appreciate what you have done. I would say, particularly you, General Cody. I got to know General Cody when he was in command of Operation Task Force Hawk, I think it was, in Bosnia, and I watched you in action there.

Chairman WARNER. Thank you very much.

At this point I would like to yield the chair to our distinguished colleague, Senator Sessions, to chair the balance of this hearing, and I call on Senator Akaka at this time. Thank you.

Senator AKAKA. Thank you, Mr. Chairman.

Dr. Chu, I am very pleased to hear that the Joint Support Operations Center will be up and operational today.

Dr. CHU. Yes, sir. The phone number actually already works.

Senator AKAKA. I understand that people will be able to contact the center by dialing a 1–888 number to get to the center. I am really delighted to hear this because it will really help families.

What did DOD do and what is it doing to promote the services provided by the center to survivors?

Dr. CHU. We are doing the following.

Senator SESSIONS [presiding]. Dr. Chu, would you yield for a second? I believe General Cody may have an engagement or a plane to catch. If he does, please know that we know you do have that challenge, and when the time comes, just let us know.

General CODY. I will hang in here until the tough questions come, Mr. Senator. [Laughter.]

I appreciate your indulgence. Thank you.

Senator SESSIONS. Dr. Chu.

Dr. CHU. Thank you, Mr. Chairman.

Senator Akaka, we are doing three things really in terms of making the service available. First, we are publicizing the existence of the center with a ceremony today and other similar steps.

Second, of course, as I would emphasize, what this center does really is build upon the individual programs of each military service, which have been described this morning. We have a significant challenge in the executive branch because, as the testimony indicates, programs come from a variety of sources, including the VA. So it is important to have a strong liaison with the VA.

Third, we are going to reach out proactively and make sure we have called everybody to ensure that they have had all their issues addressed. That will take some time. I would recognize that will not happen overnight. But we want to be sure. There is always a challenge with complex Government programs that no one falls through the cracks, that everyone understands how the various benefits and services work, and that they can take advantage of them. I think the majority do now. The Army and the Marine Corps have led the way with Marine for Life and DS3. We are just trying to make sure we have left no stone unturned in terms of the services we offer to our personnel.

Senator AKAKA. Grief services are one of the kind of services that can be given. With this center, will data be collected and utilized to provide greater grieving services to family survivors?

Dr. CHU. We would be delighted to look at that, Senator. I think on that front, I particularly want to single out, as I think Senator Dayton's comments did, what our casualty assistance officers (CAOs) already do. They are, of course, the ones who must bring the terrible news to a family first. I believe they do a superb job. They are well-trained by the military departments. Obviously, there is always an issue or two we could improve in terms of their training. But that is the first step I think in the grieving process. But we will certainly look at your issue, sir.

Senator AKAKA. Also, there has been some concern about survivors' benefits, and in particular, some have raised issues regarding the processing time for survivor benefits. Can you mention anything about processing times?

Dr. CHU. Yes, sir. As you appreciate, there really are three pillars to the annuity or income support benefits that a surviving family receives. There is the survivor benefit plan, which we have discussed. There is the VA payment, which was mentioned. There is also Social Security. Actually, about a year and a half ago, we partnered with Social Security to inaugurate a new, expedited process that we think demonstrates that can be speeded up. So it is a matter of days before that is taken care of as opposed to weeks or months.

On the SBP, that does take a little time, typically 1 to 2 months. There are some papers the family must sign. If there are children, the spouse must decide if she or he wishes to elect payment of those benefits to the children. So there are some decisions the family must make, and we try to be thoughtful about not asking them to make that decision the next day. So there is a lag built into the process, and then the payments, if I recall correctly, typically are made on a monthly basis so that it is the first of the next pay period before you are actually going to see a check. So there are some delays there. We are looking constantly at how we can improve these processes and cut down on these delays.

Senator AKAKA. I understand that some of the claims have been heavy. Are there any efforts being made to accelerate the processing time?

Dr. CHU. Yes, sir. As I indicated, we have given attention to that the last year and a half or so. We will give continuing attention to that issue. We would like to be sure the families are paid as promptly as possible.

Senator AKAKA. This question goes out to all the Service Chiefs. While I understand that the DOD is dedicating the Joint Support Operations Center today and is providing the 1–888 number to assist survivors during this difficult time, are there other areas that we should be focusing on to help in this transition?

Admiral NATHMAN. Well, sir, I would say, one area that I feel we have focused on goes back to this relationship to the CAO to the family. This does not terminate when a check is signed off or when a particular transition has occurred to the VA. I personally want to thank the VA for all they do for us in this because of the liaison work we do with them.

But there is a very strong relationship—some people would call it a bond—between the CAO and the family, and we have really focused on that. We treat it as a central activity at our Personnel Command. We make sure that the Casualty Assistance Calls Officers (CACOs) are trained. We make sure they understand that they can explain at a technical level and a basic level for the members of the family. They have a strong relationship that is sustained for as long as the family needs that sustained relationship.

I think these are the kinds of things that serve the family—we have coalesced it now on this center, but the intent I believe is already being performed at our service level, and this is just a good way now to integrate it. I think this is an important part of our service. I think it starts and, frankly, ends with the CACO because the relationship he forms with the family. No one else can do that.

Mr. EPLEY. If I could add to that. The VA has been mentioned in this. Senator, you asked if there are improvements. We do defer to the DOD CAO. We do work with him very closely, but when we get notice of the casualty or when we get a claim, we have centralized that to our Philadelphia center where we also do the insurance payments. We are paying those DIC benefits now in about 3 days on average. So we really have expedited that process by centralizing it for in-service death.

General NYLAND. I would also add that with regard to the initiatives that Dr. Chu mentioned, the expedited claims process (ECP) with both the VA and Social Security, we have seen tremendous progress in making sure that those benefits are promptly received by the surviving members. I think those initiatives, along with the initiatives that each of the Services has taken to include their CACOs and now the Joint Support Operations Center, which members of our Services will man as well so that they can turn survivors to the right source immediately, all are pointed in that right direction, sir.

General MOSELEY. Senator, our casualty assistance representative has a full-time job. That is a career field for these folks. They are not part-time, nor do they change over. These folks receive extensive training, and they interface with the VA. Let me also thank the VA for being a good partner in this. We are also exploring opportunities with the Department of Labor so that these people will develop contacts there and have visibility on things that are going on within the Department of Labor. That is a new one for us, and we are just learning what opportunities we have there.

But this comes down through all of our units down to the lowest common denominator as a squadron or a flight, and the first sergeants and the commanders and all the supervisors know that this person, this casualty assistance representative, is the point of contact for that family and the assigned person to that member for the length of his or her care.

Senator AKAKA. Thank you very much, Mr. Chairman.

Senator SESSIONS. Thank you, Senator Akaka.

In the calls I make to the families who have lost loved ones in combat, I ask how things are going. They brag on the casualty assistance officers. I have had people break down. They almost become like a member of the family. They help them and they go far beyond what you would expect them to be helping with. I think that is something that works, and I salute you for being true to your commitment to the families, as well as the men and women in uniform.

Senator Thune, it is a delight to have you on the committee. I know you wanted to be on this committee, and we are delighted that that has occurred. You served in the House and as a Senate staffer. So you hit the ground running. It is a delight to have you here and it is a pleasure for me to recognize you at this time.

Senator THUNE. Thank you, Mr. Chairman. Let me acknowledge also that since this is my first hearing as a new member of this very prestigious committee, what a privilege it is to serve on the committee and to have the opportunity to serve with you, Mr. Chairman, and other members of this committee.

The work before this committee today is perhaps the most important responsibility that falls on the shoulders of this great body, and that is our responsibility to our young men and women serving in harm's way. Because we are a country at war, the needs of our service men and women and their families must be one of our highest priorities. We cannot put a value on the sacrifice of those who have died in Iraq and Afghanistan, nor can we hope to fully compensate families for a lost husband, wife, brother, son, or daughter. But we can do more and hopefully we will. That is why I appreciate very much the hearing today.

I support raising the death gratuity from $12,000 to $100,000 for service men and women who have lost their lives in combat and also believe it ought to be retroactive to soldiers who have died fighting in the war on terrorism since September 11.

I think that about everything that can be asked about with respect to the specific legislation has been asked today, and I appreciate very much your answers and the questions of our colleagues here on the committee. I think it has shed a considerable amount of light on the issue and on the solutions that have been proposed as well.

But I would like to perhaps just ask one question with respect to something that was in the written testimony of General Nyland and perhaps get each of you to comment, if you might, with respect to your particular branch. General Nyland, you had mentioned, in discussing this whole issue of benefits, that it ultimately is part of the recruiting and retention package. In an increasingly difficult recruiting environment, particularly for the two Services that are shouldering the greatest burden of death and injury in this war, we must take a hard look at anything that will set the minds of those in the war and their families at ease.

I guess in a broader way, I am sort of curious to know what the status of our recruiting efforts is today and are we seeing young people, men and women, who are continually being attracted to serve in the military, and what, if anything, can be done to improve your ability to be able to recruit young men and women into the Service. So if you would comment generally with respect to that overall question.

General NYLAND. Yes, sir. Today our recruiting and retention are still going quite well. We are over 9 years in making our recruiting goals. Our retention rates are on track with previous years for both our first-term and second-term members.

It is however, getting more difficult. Surprisingly, more of the questions come now from the parents than from the individual. The young man or woman still wants to serve. The mother or father wants to know how will he be trained, how will he be led, when will he go.

So I think anything that helps round out the package and an understanding of what these benefits can mean certainly is going to be not only a step in the right direction, but has to at least help in the education of a member who wants to come into one of the military services to understand that there are benefits there that, God forbid, should they lose their life or have serious injury, that this country is not going to forget them.

Senator THUNE. Any others have comments on that, just on the general overall status of recruitment?

Dr. CHU. Let me, if I could, Senator, answer for the DOD. In active recruiting, as General Nyland said, the Services are making their goals. They are also doing well on retention. We do have a somewhat greater challenge on the Reserve front, I should acknowledge.

I think General Nyland touched on a very key point. There is a place in which you can help us. The military, since the first Persian Gulf war, in various public opinion polls, is the most respected institution in this country. It stayed right up there all the last 15 years. When you next ask parents, "Would you advise your son, daughter, nephew, niece, et cetera to join?" support drops. Where we need your help is in celebrating the value of military service, the values that people are going to get out of this period of service. They are going to come back a better person and a better citizen. I think that message from parents, from older siblings, uncles, aunts, school counselors, is a very important message to send to the young men and young women of America, to celebrate their choice.

General CODY. Senator, I just came back from a trip at one of our enlistment stations in Chicago. In fact, I had the great opportunity to enlist into the Army 25 of our newest soldiers. Four of them were 17 years old. None of them, when I asked them why they wanted to join onto the Army, mentioned benefits. Five or 6 years ago, you would hear about benefits and education. Most of the time now I hear our country is at war or I want to serve. Now, that does not mean that we ought to stop the benefits and the educational benefits and everything else because I think they are very important.

I also would tell you that I enlisted them in the center court of the Chicago Bulls vs. Boston Celtics game that night and it was a packed house. If you could have seen the thunderous applause of the arena that night, recognizing that these young men and women just raised their right hand to serve the Army that is at war, it was heartfelt. I would like to think that support exists throughout this country.

But that is where we need help. The influencers of these young children, young teenagers, are really their parents. I think we need to talk more about service to this Nation. In many cases, these young men and women absolutely understand it. They understand this is a calling of their time. But I think it would be helpful if we could get some more help with the influencers, who are their parents, and what service to our Nation means, and also the fact that when we take these young men and women in no matter what service, we are committed to giving them great leadership, but we will also let them reach their full potential. I think that is a story that we need to continue to harp on.

General MOSELEY. Senator, let me agree with everything my colleagues have said, but add a couple of thoughts for you. It is axiomatic in the retention world that you recruit the member but you retain the family. So anything that we can do to make that bond tighter will benefit all of us because it is the family that is important while our members are away. These deployment numbers—the Air Force experienced about a 500-percent higher deployment rate than we did in the early 1990s. So our members are away from families at a much higher rate and they are away longer than they have been before. So you do recruit that member, but you retain that family. That is a big deal for us.

Also, all of these things that we are talking today in this hearing are critically important for us because it is an article of faith for our people. When they take the oath to defend the Republic, it is an article of faith that the Republic will stand by them.

Senator Sessions, thank you so much for what you are asking of us today, and Senator, I would only add those two things to my colleagues.

Admiral NATHMAN. Senator, I would add that on the recruiting side, the Navy is on a path of reshaping its force. We are reshaping our recruiting goals as a result of that because we are going to downsize. At the same time, we want to attract the best and the brightest to our Service, and I think the most important point about attracting the best and the brightest to our Service is that we sustain the value of serving. What I find very pleasing in this discussion today is it has all been about sustaining the value of service. That is really important in this discussion. In the near term, the most important thing we can do to sustain that value is win this fight in Iraq.

Senator THUNE. I appreciate very much your answers to those questions and would just say that as a new member of this committee—and I think all my colleagues on the committee—would also welcome any suggestion that you have with respect to pay, benefits, compensation, and all those things that continue to make service in the military attractive, in addition to the things that you have mentioned about creating this culture and celebrating the work that they do. It is so important. We are very grateful and proud of the work they do. So thank you for your testimony.

Senator SESSIONS. Senator Clinton.

Senator CLINTON. Thank you very much. I want to thank the chairman for holding this hearing. I think it is a subject that is not only very important but needs to be addressed, and I am delighted we are doing so.

Last week I joined with Senator Chuck Hagel in introducing legislation to raise the survivor benefit from $12,000 to $100,000, and I am delighted the administration will be making such recommendations. The legislation we introduced would have been retroactive to November 2001, and I think that it is very important that it be so.

I have also joined the efforts led by Senators Sessions and Lieberman. These are reforms that I think send the right signal about the sustainability of service and the respect and regard we have for those who do serve.

Several other issues have been raised in this hearing, and I appreciate very much Chairman Warner's concern that we address all of them and this gives us an opportunity to do so.

General Cody, I appreciate your comments about following up on the soldiers who have been injured. I recently had occasion to write to the Secretary of the Army with respect to a case that came to my attention in New York of Specialist Lauria who is an amputee who was at Walter Reed and was presented with a significant bill and was going to have his pay docked. In our efforts to look into this, we discovered that there were at least, I think, 19 other soldiers in a similar situation. I understand a task force was created at Fort Hood. I have not yet received an answer to my letter to the Secretary—and I would very much appreciate receiving that—to look at issues of payment and debt arising out of service and service-connected disabilities and how we best treat those.

Another issue that I think is significant, which has been alluded to today, is this question about military insurance. There was a series of articles in the New York Times last year detailing how many servicemembers were being taken advantage of by unscrupulous insurance agents who were selling soldiers insurance that offered high cost but little return. Mr. Chairman, I would ask unanimous consent to place those articles in the record.

Senator SESSIONS. Without objection, they will be made a part of the record.

[The New York Times articles follow:]

The New York Times October 19, 2004 Tuesday

The New York Times

October 19, 2004 Tuesday
Late Edition - Final

SECTION: Section C; Column 4; Business/Financial Desk; Pg. 3

LENGTH: 440 words

HEADLINE: Subpoena Issued to Insurer Over Sales to G.I.'s

BYLINE: By DIANA B. HENRIQUES

BODY:

The American Amicable Life Insurance Company of Waco, Tex., confirmed yesterday that the Justice Department had subpoenaed documents relating to the company's sale of insurance products to military personnel and other federal employees.

The civil subpoena -- which people who participated in discussions about it said was issued by the United States attorney's office in Philadelphia -- was served in late July, after a series in The New York Times disclosed that the company's agents had used misleading sales practices to sell expensive life insurance policies to Iraq-bound recruits at Fort Benning, Ga.

"The company is working with the Department of Justice regarding a civil inquiry," said Mark Palmer, a company spokesman. "Our desire is to responsibly respond to the U.S. attorney's questions while continuing to provide solid, stable life insurance to our customers."

A company memorandum obtained by The New York Times showed that the subpoena specifically asked for information about the decision to begin selling "any company product as a savings plan rather than as an insurance plan or policy."

Last month, American Amicable of Texas dismissed three agents involved in the abusive sales at Fort Benning, disciplined a fourth agent and offered to return premiums that soldiers there paid for their policies -- $1,200 a year for death benefits of less than $30,000. Several young soldiers who bought the policies said they thought they had enrolled in a savings or investment plan.

Michael S. Blume, an assistant United States attorney in Philadelphia, said yesterday that his office "can't confirm or deny the existence of any investigation, as a matter of policy."

American Amicable Life Insurance is one of four companies owned by American Amicable Holding, also based in Waco. Last year, its sister company, Pioneer American Insurance Company quietly offered refunds to more than 340 marines at Camp Pendleton, Calif., after base legal officers complained about misleading sales tactics.

Additional refunds may be owed to soldiers at other bases where the agents at Fort Benning also worked, according to insurance regulators in Georgia, who are conducting a broad investigation of insurance sales on military bases in that state.

This month, the nation's leading insurance ratings agency, A.M. Best Company, announced that it was reviewing, with negative implications, the financial strength ratings of the American Amicable Holding affiliates based on "the adverse publicity within the military base life insurance market surrounding improper sales practices by some agents with enlisted military personnel."

The New York Times October 6, 2004 Wednesday

The New York Times

October 6, 2004 Wednesday
Late Edition - Final

SECTION: Section C; Column 4; Business/Financial Desk; Pg. 6

LENGTH: 964 words

HEADLINE: House Moves to Protect G.I.'s on Finances

BYLINE: By DIANA B. HENRIQUES

BODY:

On a broadly bipartisan vote, the House of Representatives approved a measure yesterday aimed at preventing marketing practices that have exposed military personnel, especially young recruits and junior officers, to high-pressure or misleading sales pitches for financial products that may not fit their financial needs.

The bill, which easily passed the House, would abolish an archaic form of mutual funds sold almost exclusively to military personnel. The funds, known as contractual plans, impose sales fees that eat up half of an investor's contributions in the first year.

The measure would also give state insurance regulators clearer jurisdiction over sales on military bases, and would require the Defense Department to establish a central registry for tracking insurance agents who violate military rules and to report the agents to state licensing agencies.

As the bill was being approved in the House, matching legislation was being prepared for introduction in the Senate by Michael B. Enzi, Republican of Wyoming, and Hillary Rodham Clinton, Democrat of New York. Other influential senators who have expressed interest in the issue include the chairman of the Senate Banking Committee, Richard C. Shelby, an Alabama Republican, and the committee's ranking Democrat, Paul S. Sarbanes of Maryland.

Approval of the bill, on a vote of 396 to 2, came less than a month after it was introduced by Representative Max Burns, a Republican of Georgia, who said his initiative was largely prompted by a series that began in July in The New York Times documenting abusive sales practices and unsuitable financial products on several military bases, including Fort Benning in Georgia.

The bill's pace reflected the support of Representative Michael G. Oxley, the chairman of the House Financial Services Committee, who arranged a hearing on it within two days of its introduction. Mr. Oxley said yesterday that the measure would help "put an end to the longstanding problem of unscrupulous securities and life insurance firms who have been taking financial advantage of the men and women in our armed forces."

Representative Rahm Emanuel, the Illinois Democrat who had first requested hearings on the issues raised by the series in The Times, had proposed a broader bill that would have doubled, from $250,000 to $500,000, the amount of low-cost life insurance available to service members through the military. But Mr. Emanuel acknowledged that his proposal would have faced more legislative hurdles than the Burns bill.

"We made choices so that this bill wouldn't get bogged down," he said of the committee's deliberations. "These were really parliamentary differences, not policy differences."

The measure has the support of state insurance regulators. "This is definitely something that needs to happen, and the House has shown real leadership in moving it as quickly as it did," said Gregory V. Serio, the superintendent of insurance for New York State and the chairman of the governmental affairs task force of the National Association of Insurance Commissioners. "I am hoping the same thing will happen in the Senate."

From a financial perspective, the most interesting feature of the Burns measure is its abolition of the high-fee mutual funds known as contractual plans, under which investors sign up to make small, monthly contributions to a mutual fund over a decade or more but pay their sales fees upfront.

The plans have been prone to sales abuses since their introduction in the 1930's. In 1966, after a string of scandals, federal securities regulators unsuccessfully urged Congress to abolish the plans. Instead, Congress imposed a grace period during which investors could cancel the plans and recover at least some of their sales charges, making the plans less attractive to brokers.

By the mid-1980's, contractual plans had virtually disappeared from the civilian market. But they continued to be promoted in the military market, most prominently by First Command Financial Planning of Fort Worth, which has sold hundreds of thousands of the plans to young servicemen and women.

The company has urged Congress to extend the grace period for investors, rather than ban the plan, said Paul Cozby, director of corporate communications for First Command. But it strongly supports the creation of a central registry to track predatory agents. And it has proposed as well that all junior enlisted personnel meet with a trained independent counselor on base before signing up for any financial products that would affect their take-home pay. It also favors a requirement that companies provide information on the rate at which their products lapse or are canceled as a condition of being allowed to sell those products on military bases.

The American Council of Life Insurers, which supported the Burns bill, has also urged that insurers that sell on military bases be required to join the Insurance Marketplace Standards Association, a voluntary industry organization that sets admission standards for its members and monitors their sales practices.

The Pentagon's own proposals for revising its rules for on-base insurance sales are expected to become public soon, Pentagon officials said. Congress, however, has blocked their implementation until the completion of a broad study of the military financial marketplace by the Government Accountability Office.

John M. Molino, the deputy under secretary of defense for military community and family policy, said there was "some dovetailing" between the bill and proposals he wants to implement, particularly in tracking rogue agents. "This will provide greater awareness across the department and among the services, and that is good news for service members and their families," he said yesterday.

The New York Times October 2, 2004 Saturday

The New York Times

October 2, 2004 Saturday
Late Edition - Final

SECTION: Section A; Column 3; Business/Financial Desk; Pg. 1

LENGTH: 2061 words

HEADLINE: Inquiry Stymied on Company With Air Force Ties

BYLINE: By DIANA B. HENRIQUES

BODY:

If you're a military officer, you can't miss First Command Financial Planning of Fort Worth.

It sells life insurance and investments to young officers serving around the world. Many of its executives and most of its agents were officers once themselves, and they let you know it. A parade of retired generals and admirals serve on its advisory boards. With more than 300,000 customers, virtually all of them current or former officers, the company depends on the military for its very existence.

And in a smaller way the military relies on First Command. The company, like others in this market, has long sponsored popular events like the Marine Corps Marathon and the Air Force talent show, Tops in Blue.

So First Command was not happy a year ago when it discovered that a legal office at Air Force headquarters had put out a notice asking military lawyers in the field for feedback on "reports of possible unethical or overly aggressive" sales practices by the company's agents. The notice also raised questions about the suitability of the company's core product, an archaic and expensive type of mutual fund with sales fees that eat up half of an investor's first-year contributions.

First Command fought back: it complained to the second- most-powerful general in the Air Force. And it was heard.

The New York Times has found that within three weeks of the legal office's posting, the Air Force issued a retraction, which it had allowed the company to edit. It gave the company a letter of exoneration, signed by the Air Force's top legal officer, after letting the company edit that, too. The Air Force legal staff stopped cooperating with a securities industry investigation into the company's practices and products. And the Air Force effectively abandoned a broad inquiry of its own, letting local base authorities handle complaints.

One complaint was about a First Command agent who had made veiled threats against a young officer in Charleston, S.C., suggesting he could be court-martialed or sued for criticizing the company in an e-mail message.

First Command's success in its face-off with Air Force lawyers was a stark illustration of how a company with strong military connections can influence the very people who are supposed to monitor its sales activities on bases.

One of those who felt that influence was Thomas L. Farmer, who, from his Pentagon office, worked on the First Command inquiry for the Judge Advocate General's Corps, which oversees the administration of justice and ethics for the Air Force. Mr. Farmer, who was a major at the time but has since left the service, said that neither the Air Force nor the company has acknowledged the chilling impact that the episode, especially the company-edited retraction, has had in the ranks.

"Most JAG officers would take it as an endorsement of First Command," Mr. Farmer said of the retraction. "Our being rebuked sends a message out to the field that 'well, they're not going to be able to help us' when it comes to this company." He added, "When we tried to tackle it, First Command could contact a four-star general and stop us, to the point where First Command is helping to write official Air Force material."

Mercer Bullard, president of Fund Democracy, an advocacy group for mutual fund shareholders' interests, said the episode underscored the danger of relying on the military to police the sale of financial products on bases.

"The JAG Corps is the most independent, most likely agency in the military to stand up to these companies," said Professor Bullard, who teaches law at the University of Mississippi. "If the JAG Corps can't do it, no one else in the military will be able to."

First Command maintains that in appealing to the top ranks of the Air Force, it was seeking fair treatment, not special treatment.

"What was put in that posting was inaccurate and unfair and harmed our company," said Lanny J. Davis, a Washington lawyer and former special counsel to the Clinton administration who represents the company. "Because we were concerned with getting a correction quickly, we couldn't afford the luxury of going up the chain of command to get a remedy. So we went as high as we could, to get it immediately."

The company went as high as Gen. T. Michael Moseley, the Air Force vice chief of staff. An Air Force spokesman, Col. Gary Halbert, said the general's role was "fairly routine," intended only to ensure that the company got a prompt and appropriate response. General Moseley, the colonel said, did not intend to discourage the Judge Advocate General's Corps from enforcing the rules that govern the sale of insurance and investments on military bases.

General Moseley himself said in a written statement: "Fighting and winning the global war on terrorism and providing support for our airmen are my top priorities. We have made and will continue to make every effort to protect our airmen from unscrupulous salespeople and fraudulent products."

Straight to the Generals

Three events prompted Mr. Farmer's office, the legal assistance and preventive law division, to send out the notice inquiring about First Command. The first was an e-mail message in early July 2003 from Vandenberg Air Force Base in California complaining that some First Command agents were using a senior officer's name without permission to get clerks to give them the telephone numbers of officer trainees.

A few weeks later, a brigadier general in the Air National Guard sent Mr. Farmer's unit a copy of an article from Kiplinger's Personal Finance magazine that criticized the expensive kind of mutual fund sold by First Command. Then the office received a request for information from NASD, the securities industry regulatory group, which had opened an inquiry into First Command.

The newsletter item, which also told field offices how to forward complaints to NASD, ran on Aug. 20, 2003, in the Judge Advocate General's Corps internal electronic newsletter, The On-Line News. And it caught the attention of the Air Force unit in San Antonio that oversees Tops in Blue, the touring Air Force talent show. Two days later, the program office asked First Command about the item. This was apparently the first the company had heard of it.

A spokesman for the judge advocate general, Lt. Col. Doug Murdock, said the item should never have gone beyond the JAG Corps. "Unfortunately," he said, "the article was interpreted as an indictment of First Command's business practices."

Lamar C. Smith, First Command's chairman and chief executive, was quick to respond. In an electronic memorandum titled "Thoughts," he acknowledged that the agent's threatening call to the young officer in Charleston "was an error and I will apologize for it." But he also expressed his anger, adding, "we have a real grievance" against the officer.

"Shall we pursue our own remedies?" Mr. Smith wrote. "If we do it will get harsh and expensive for the officer in a hurry."

The memo was sent to the Air Force by a senior vice president, Kurt B. Anderson, a retired Air Force general. A copy was obtained by The Times, as were copies of other documents for this article, including e-mail messages and handwritten notes of telephone conversations. Both the Air Force and First Command verified the authenticity of the documents.

Mr. Davis, the company's lawyer, said Mr. Smith's "Thoughts" had been written in the heat of the moment. But he acknowledged that Mr. Smith had been "upset and frustrated" with the Air Force and conveyed those feelings to senior officers.

One of them, the company said, was an old friend of Mr. Smith, Gen. Richard Brown 3rd, now retired, who was the acting assistant vice chief of staff. Mr. Smith then sent a letter of outrage to General Moseley, who had just become vice chief of staff. The letter, dated Aug. 28, cited the company's long support for Tops in Blue, condemned the Kiplinger's article and complained that the JAG item's author was "inviting others to join his war on First Command by filing complaints with regulators."

What the JAG staff should have done, Mr. Smith said, was report the Vandenberg complaint and any others to First Command.

The company would then have taken "instant and withering" action to discipline any agent involved, Mr. Smith wrote. He demanded that the JAG office run a "crystal clear retraction" and advise officers in the field that the item "should be disregarded."

The Order Is Retracted

A week later, the company said, another senior First Command executive, Rich Giles, a former Air Force captain, telephoned General Moseley, whom he had known for 30 years. And on Sept. 5, Mr. Smith followed up with a second letter to General Moseley warning that the company faced "the early stages of a 'wild fire.'"

Mr. Smith's complaint moved down the chain of command from General Moseley to the judge advocate general, Thomas J. Fiscus. Two days later, General Fiscus called a staff member at home and loudly upbraided him for his staff's handling of the First Command inquiry, notes in the JAG files show. He cited the letters and calls to General Moseley and warned of possible litigation.

Colonel Murdock, the JAG spokesman, said the general was "reacting to his discovery that there were very limited complaints" behind the office's original inquiry.

The staff was now directed to draft a retraction for the newsletter. But its language did not satisfy General Anderson, the First Command executive, who was allowed to edit the item. His version, published almost verbatim on Sept. 10, 2003, said that "virtually no negative information about First Command has been received" as a result of the original item.

First Command was allowed to edit the retraction because the Air Force believed that was appropriate "to resolve the unfair impact" of the item, Colonel Murdock said.

On Sept. 18, First Command got the letter of exoneration it had demanded. The letter, too, was edited by the company, Colonel Murdock said. One change, though small, was significant. The Air Force's draft said the original item had been prompted by "complaints." First Command proposed changing that to "a single complaint." Lt. Col. Timothy Guiden, Mr. Farmer's boss, opposed the change, noting that four problems had been reported. He was overruled, the documents show.

The letter "tried to correct the record for their customers, undo any harm that had been done and level the playing field," Colonel Murdock said. But military documents confirm that complaints continued to arrive, both in writing and made orally to General Fiscus. (He temporarily stepped down last week pending the outcome of an unrelated Air Force investigation.) In each complaint, agents appeared to be trying to use "command influence," the power of senior leaders to sway junior officers, on First Command's behalf.

Only the incidents at Vandenberg and Charleston were ever reported to First Command, the company said. Its only disciplinary response was to counsel the agent in Charleston, said Mr. Davis, the company's lawyer. The Air Force said that none of the other complaints had revealed any systemic problem and that all had been resolved at the local base level. None were passed along to NASD, either.

"After we got slapped down in such a public manner, continued cooperation with the NASD was off the table," Mr. Farmer said.

NASD has nevertheless pursued its inquiry, which has been joined by the Securities and Exchange Commission and should be concluded soon, Congressional aides say.

Since The Times first examined First Command's practices in a two-part series in July, the company has come under scrutiny in Congress. Lawmakers are considering legislation to abolish the type of mutual funds the company sells and require the military to coordinate more closely with civilian regulators.

There was one small coda. In January, First Command notified the Air Force that it would no longer provide $150,000 a year to sponsor Tops in Blue. The company said the decision was based on "marketing considerations." But one Air Force executive attributed the loss directly to the JAG office's initial newsletter query about First Command. In an e-mail message to General Fiscus last Jan. 30, the executive wrote: "This is 'water under the bridge' but wanted you to know the consequences of the article."

URL: http://www.nytimes.com

GRAPHIC: Photos: Members of the Air Force musical ensemble Tops in Blue at a performance last year in Montgomery, Ala. The group was sponsored by First Command Financial Planning of Fort Worth until last January. (Photo by Karen S. Doerr/Montgomery

Advertiser/Associated Press)(pg. C2)Chart: "Damage Control"On Aug. 20, 2003, responding to concerns from the field, the Air Force Judge Advocate General's Corps sent out an internal message seeking feedback on any sales abuses by First Command Financial Planning, a firm that caters to military officers. Three weeks later, the Air Force retracted that message. Heres what happened:THE PLAYERSFirst CommandFinancial PlanningGEN. KURT B. ANDERSON (AIR FORCE, RETIRED)Senior vice presidentLAMAR C. SMITHChief executiveUnited States Air ForceGEN. T. MICHAEL MOSELEYVice chief of staffGEN. THOMAS J. FISCUS*Judge advocate generalCHAIN OF EVENTSVoicing a complaintAfter consulting with another general, Mr. Smith writes General Moseley two letters demanding a retraction.Mr. Smith also tells former General Anderson, a First Command executive, to be his liaison with General Fiscus on the issue.Drafting a correctionGeneral Moseley forwards First Commands complaints to General Fiscus for immediate action.General Fiscus agrees to provide the retraction and orders his staff to work up a draft.Reviewing and rewritingGeneral Fiscus sends the draft to General Anderson at First Command for review.General Anderson, along with Mr. Smith, substantially revise the draft.Approving the final draftGeneral Anderson sends the edited retraction back to General Fiscus.General Fiscus approves the edited version of the retraction and it is published in the JAG staffs weekly newsletter.FINAL VERSIONRetraction as it ran in the Sept. 10, 2003, JAG newsletter.LANGUAGE ADDED OR CHANGED BY FIRST COMMAND*Stepped down Sept. 22 pending an unrelated Air Force investigation(Sources by Air Force files
interviews with First Command Financial Planning and the Air Force)(pg. C2)

The New York Times September 23, 2004 Thursday Correction Appended

The New York Times

September 23, 2004 Thursday
Correction Appended
Late Edition - Final

SECTION: Section C; Column 3; Business/Financial Desk; Pg. 1

LENGTH: 1019 words

HEADLINE: Insurer to Refund Money To Soldiers Who Bought High-Cost Life Policies

BYLINE: By DIANA B. HENRIQUES

BODY:

Hundreds of soldiers who unwittingly signed up for high-cost life insurance during basic training at Fort Benning, Ga., will receive full cash refunds from the insurance company whose agents sold the policies, a spokesman for the company confirmed yesterday.

And those refunds may be just the beginning, according to a state insurance regulator who is investigating whether similar refunds may be justified for soldiers who bought policies at other bases in Georgia.

The refunds, unusual in the insurance market, are being offered by the American Amicable Life Insurance Company of Waco, Tex.

Three agents who sold the policies have been dismissed by the company, and a fourth has resigned, according to a spokesman, Mark Palmer.

The refunds are being coordinated with the Georgia insurance commissioner, who said yesterday that his continuing investigation of military insurance sales has now widened to include at least four other insurers selling on military bases in that state.

The insurance commissioner, John W. Oxendine, said his staff had decided to make formal "market conduct" examinations of Pioneer American Life Insurance, a sister company to American Amicable in Waco; Trans World Assurance of San Mateo, Calif.; an affiliate, the American Fidelity Life Insurance Company of Pensacola, Fla.; and the Madison National Life Insurance Company of Middleton, Wis.

Fred Graefe, a lawyer for Trans World and American Fidelity, said yesterday that the companies had "been in close contact" with the Georgia insurance department for several weeks and had "complied fully with all its requests."

The administrative support staff for both companies, in Pensacola, is still digging out from the devastation of Hurricane Ivan last week, he said, but hope to be able to deal with any additional requests from regulators soon.

Larry Graber, the president of Madison National, said yesterday that he had not yet received any formal notice of a market conduct inquiry by the Georgia regulators, but that he would check into it.

Mr. Oxendine said the Georgia department was also "discussing the appropriateness" of American Amicable offering refunds to soldiers at other bases in Georgia, but he cautioned that refunds alone would not "get them off the hook" with regulators. "There is also the issue of appropriate punishment," he said, "and making sure that this does not happen again."

Mr. Oxendine's investigation was begun in late July as a result of a series in The New York Times on the problems of abusive sales practices and unsuitable insurance and investment products in the military market.

He said he could not estimate when it might conclude, because it is "growing broader and deeper every day."

News of the pending refunds by American Amicable was greeted with cheers by some of the soldiers who purchased the policies in late 2002 and early 2003 at classroom briefings on financial management during their basic training at Fort Benning.

"It is fair, first of all, and well deserved by the soldiers who were misled into investing in this stuff," said Army Specialist Brendan Conger of Fort Bragg, N.C., who recently testified about his experience at Fort Benning before a Congressional subcommittee. "I'm a soldier 24/7, and there just wouldn't have been any time for me to go through the process of trying to get my money back on my own."

Specialist Nicholas Stachler, who also serves at Fort Bragg, said he was "completely and utterly excited" about the refunds. "I thought it was going to be a long drawn-out thing," he said yesterday. "It's just really cool that it went through. It's awesome."

It is also fairly unusual, at least on this scale, said Joseph M. Belth, emeritus professor of insurance at Indiana University and editor of The Insurance Forum, an independent periodical.

"Certainly, it is out of the ordinary to be giving refunds out to that many people, firstly, and, secondly, without any legal action on the part of the policyholders," he said.

The Georgia investigation "also raises all kinds of questions about what's going on in the rest of the country," he added, noting that other state commissioners should be examining practices at their own military bases as well.

Hundreds of young soldiers could be eligible for the refunds on the Fort Benning policies, people working on the plan said, although the exact number and the amount of money involved have not been determined.

Many young soldiers, like Specialists Stachler and Conger, had $100 a month in premiums deducted from their paychecks for the policies during their yearlong tours of duty in Iraq last year. For them, the refunds could total more than $1,200, or about a month's base salary for soldiers in the lowest ranks.

"I'm very pleased, and applaud American Amicable Life Insurance for doing the right and just thing," said Pamela Stachler, Specialist Stachler's mother, in Athens, Ohio. "However, there needs to be policies in place with our military so this does not happen anymore, not even one more time."

The search for legislative ways to prevent future problems is continuing in Congress, where the House Financial Services Committee is considering legislation to address the problem.

And yesterday, the Republican chairman and the ranking Democrat on the Senate Banking

Committee added their names to the growing roster of lawmakers asking the Government Accountability Office to examine aspects of the issue.

The accountability office is already working on an examination of the military financial services market. But the two senators -- the banking committee chairman, Richard C. Shelby, an Alabama Republican, and Paul S. Sarbanes, a Maryland Democrat -- asked the G.A.O. to broaden that study further.

Specifically, the senators asked that the audit agency assess the regulatory oversight that governs the sale of financial products on military installations, compare those protections with those in the civilian marketplace and rate the quality and variety of financial products being sold on military bases.

URL: http://www.nytimes.com

CORRECTION-DATE: September 25, 2004

CORRECTION:

An article in Business Day on Thursday about an insurance company's plans to give refunds to soldiers who bought high-cost policies at Fort Benning, Ga., misstated the given name of one soldier. He is Specialist Brandon Conger, not Brendan.

GRAPHIC: Photos: Nicholas Stachler, left, said he was "completely and utterly excited" about the refunds. His former roommate, Michael Fresenbeurg, right, discussed the paperwork with him. (Photo by Linda Spillers for The New York Times)(pg. C1)
Specialist Brendan Conger, left, said he would not have had the time to pursue a refund on his own. Joe W. Dunlap, an executive at American Amicable Life, right, testified before a Congressional panel. (Photographs by Carol T. Powers for The New York Times)(pg. C4)

The New York Times September 10, 2004 Friday

The New York Times

September 10, 2004 Friday
Late Edition - Final

SECTION: Section C; Column 3; Business/Financial Desk; Pg. 3

LENGTH: 1249 words

HEADLINE: Hearing Confronts Insurers Who Market to Soldiers

BYLINE: By DIANA B. HENRIQUES

DATELINE: WASHINGTON, Sept. 9

BODY:

The chairman of a House subcommittee that is investigating the sale of life insurance and mutual funds to young soldiers and other military members unleashed a scathing attack on Thursday on financial companies active on military bases. The chairman, Representative Richard H. Baker, Republican of Louisiana, challenged not only the sales practices of their agents but also the fundamental merits of their products.

Mr. Baker led a four-hour hearing through a review of how life insurance and mutual funds are sold on military bases, opening with testimony from Specialist Brandon Conger, a soldier who said he was misled into buying an expensive insurance policy he did not want or understand, and ending with promises of swift, bipartisan action to address the problems.

Mr. Baker questioned whether the life insurance industry had done enough to root out agents who prey on young soldiers and indicated that the Pentagon might have a future date with Congress to explain its failure to adequately police the agents it allows on bases.

But Mr. Baker's fiercest criticisms fell on the companies that package and sell the high-commission products. He singled out the complex form of insurance sold to Specialist Conger by the American Amicable Life Insurance Company in Waco, Tex., and a type of mutual fund marketed by First Command Financial Services, in Fort Worth.

The product combines an expensive insurance policy that provides a low death benefit with an interest-earning savings fund that can accumulate cash value over 20 years. The mutual fund, called a contractual plan, imposes sales charges that consume half of an investor's first-year contributions.

Mr. Baker relentlessly questioned whether either product was ever suitable for military families living on fairly limited means. His doubts were echoed by the leader of a mutual fund shareholders' group and by the president of a national group of financial planners, both of whom said that far more appropriate options were available to help military families achieve the same insurance and investment goals.

Executives of both companies defended their products, saying that they are appropriate and intended to allow members of the military to accumulate retirement savings.

Joe Dunlap, executive vice president for American Amicable, said that it was unfair to compare his company's Horizon Life product -- which charges $900 in first-year premiums for death benefits of $20,950 -- with forms of insurance that do not provide cash accumulation. He said the product was intended to supplement, not replace, a soldier's low-cost military insurance, which provides $250,000 in death benefits for premiums of about $240 a year.

But that argument was challenged at the hearing by Elizabeth W. Jetton, an independent financial planner in Atlanta and the president of the Financial Planning Association.

Cash-value life insurance "is often pitched as a retirement solution," Ms. Jetton said. "In the case of the military in particular, we believe this approach is misguided and misleading. The primary rationale for purchasing life insurance must be to protect one's family from the economic consequences of the breadwinner's death. Any reference to retirement planning only confuses the issue."

Specialist Conger, a member of the 82nd Airborne Division who served in Iraq and is now at Fort Bragg, N.C., acknowledged that he had confused the insurance policy he bought with a mutual fund.

"This has been an extremely disappointing ordeal for me and for some of my fellow soldiers," Specialist Conger said. He was upset, he said, not because he lost money but because he had been misled by former soldiers who used their contacts "to gain the trust and confidence of young soldiers."

The chief executive of First Command, Lamar C. Smith, agreed that the rules governing contractual plans could be changed to give investors who withdraw early a larger refund of sales fees. But he said that the discipline that the high fees imposed had helped thousands of First Command customers in the military to build substantial assets.

"These plans are only recommended to investors who have long-term goals for wealth accumulation -- such as most of our clients -- who will likely enjoy many years of steady employment," Mr. Smith said, noting that the company's customers express a very high level of satisfaction with the service.

Mr. Baker and several other members of the capital markets subcommittee of the House Financial Services Committee repeatedly expressed doubts that the fee structure of contractual plans, which have been around since 1930 but have virtually disappeared from the civilian fund market, made them suitable for any investor, especially military families of limited means.

"The question we need to ask ourselves today is: If contractual mutual funds are such a great product, why aren't they sold to civilians anymore?" said Representative Rahm Emanuel, Democrat of Illinois.

Representative Max Burns, Republican of Georgia, who was invited to join the subcommittee that held the hearing, asked Ms. Jetton whether she thought it was ever suitable to recommend contractual plans to investors. She answered: "I really cannot think of the time when there is not a better alternative that will address more efficiently the goals these plans are supposed to address."

Both Mr. Emanuel and Mr. Burns have proposed legislation that would prohibit the sale of contractual plans and strengthen state regulation of on-base insurance marketing. Mr. Emanuel's proposal would also raise to $500,000 the amount of coverage available under the military's low-cost insurance plan. In addition, Representative Steve Israel, Democrat of New York, has proposed legislation that would require the Pentagon to pay for that low-cost insurance.

Mercer Bullard, the founder of Fund Democracy, a fund shareholders' advocacy group, said a simpler way for Congress to deal with contractual plans would be to repeal the parts of federal law that have exempted the plans from the limits that securities regulators already impose on other mutual fund fees.

It will be far more difficult, Mr. Bullard said, to end the abusive sales practices that regularly crop up in the military market. "The insulated command nature of the military life is a double-edged sword," Mr. Bullard said. "It creates a unique opportunity for government to protect our soldiers from abusive sales practices. But for sales people, it provides the opportunity to more easily exploit unsophisticated investors."

The only way to stamp out sales abuses on military bases is for the Pentagon to change the way it deals with those incidents, argued Frank Keating, the former governor of Oklahoma and the president of the American Council of Life Insurers. He called on the Pentagon to set up a central command that would oversee financial services, handle complaints, administer investigations and act as a liaison with the appropriate state and federal regulators.

Only then, he said, can incidents like the one Specialist Conger experienced become more than "an isolated incident receiving an arbitrary evaluation." When a complaint is made to multiple regulators and to multiple base commanders, he said, "it could result in license revocation or penalties that sting."

"The cracks in the system become sealed and this behavior is rooted out, not to find fertile ground on another installation or in another state or foreign country," Mr. Keating said.

URL: http://www.nytimes.com

GRAPHIC: Photos: Lamar Smith, left, chief of First Command Financial Planning, and Joe Dunlap, executive vice president of American Amicable Life Insurance. (Photo by Carol T. Powers for The New York Times)
Specialist Brandon Conger testified before the subcommittee that is investigating insurance sales. (Photo by Carol T. Powers for The New York Times)

The New York Times September 8, 2004 Wednesday

The New York Times

September 8, 2004 Wednesday
Late Edition - Final

SECTION: Section C; Column 2; Business/Financial Desk; Pg. 1

LENGTH: 1991 words

HEADLINE: Deepening Debate on Soldiers and Insurers

BYLINE: By DIANA B. HENRIQUES

BODY:

In May 2002, a young, unmarried soldier named Michael R. Deuel, serving with the 82nd Airborne division at Fort Bragg, N.C., signed up to pay nearly $120 a month for life insurance that supplemented the much less expensive coverage he had through the military.

But before he shipped out for Iraq, Private Deuel called to cancel some of his coverage because an officer on base "told him he did not need it," according to an insurance agent who served the base. A year later, in June 2003, the 21-year-old soldier was shot and killed while guarding a propane distribution center in Baghdad.

The case of Private Deuel is one of five incidents that some life insurers and their agents have offered as proof that improper meddling by senior officers is preventing young soldiers from getting supplemental insurance coverage before they head for dangerous duty abroad. By their account, thousands of other people in the military -- one insurance marketing executive puts the number as high as 6,000 -- have had similar experiences and are at risk of sharing Private Deuel's fate. The complaints have led to an investigation by the Government Accountability Office.

But an examination of the five cases in which young soldiers said they were dropping their insurance on an officer's advice and were later killed on duty shows that the issue is not so simple. The insurance being sold to the soldiers included policies that provided little additional coverage at high prices.

Four of the cases illustrate a little-noticed sales technique used by many insurance agents -- selling military people an expensive policy in tandem with a low-cost policy. Agents who complain that soldiers have been wrongly advised to cancel policies do not distinguish between the two types of insurance. In fact, Private Deuel canceled only a policy that would have cost him $100 a month for a death benefit of $32,500, while keeping a $250,000 policy that cost him $18.75 a month.

Financial experts say that in most cases young Iraq-bound soldiers would be well advised to avoid the more costly policies, which include a savings plan as well as a death benefit, and stay with the less expensive ones, especially if they have young families.

But the insurance industry says soldiers, not their officers, should have the final say. Officers who advise troops to cancel their supplemental insurance "are hypocritical 'insurance gods' who advise lower and younger service people, who statistically are the ones losing their lives in war and are in harm's way, not to buy additional life insurance," said Richard L. Worsham of Hopkinsville, Ky., a marketing director who oversees more than 150 insurance agents serving military bases in eight Southern states and who lobbied for the G.A.O. investigation.

Mr. Worsham defended the more expensive products his agents sell as a useful retirement savings tool.

The American Council of Life Insurers, the industry's trade group, has encouraged any member companies with similar complaints about officer interference to notify the G.A.O., a spokesman said yesterday. And the issue may be raised in questioning tomorrow at a House subcommittee hearing examining whether young recruits are being exposed to high-pressure or misleading sales pitches, he said.

All service members can buy up to $250,000 in low-cost life insurance through the military, and 96 percent of them buy the maximum coverage, currently $16.25 a month. Some soldiers -- those with young families or siblings, for instance -- may want additional coverage, especially if they expect to serve in dangerous places.

But among the five soldiers cited by Mr. Worsham as having bought and then dropped their supplemental insurance, four of them -- including Private Deuel -- had actually applied for two different types of insurance, sold by the same agents at the same time, according to the application forms and other documentation provided by Mr. Worsham.

One was a simple, low-cost insurance policy offered through the Military Benefit Association, a nonprofit organization in Chantilly, Va. That policy, which pays a very low commission to the agents who sell it, gave Private Deuel $250,000 in supplemental coverage for $18.75 a month, $2.50 more than the premiums on the same coverage under his military plan. Financial planners and insurance experts say this form of coverage, called term insurance, is a good bargain for young soldiers of limited means who are seeking more coverage than they can buy through the military.

The other policy for which Private Deuel signed up was a Flexible Dollar Builder policy from the Trans World Assurance Company in San Mateo, Calif. This complex product, a form of "cash value" insurance, combines a small, expensive death benefit with an "accumulation fund" feature that allows policyholders to build interest-earning savings over time. That second policy would have cost Private Deuel $100 a month for a death benefit of $32,500.

This policy pays a large front-end commission to the selling agent. But its financial benefits to the policyholder accrue more slowly. Indeed, in most cases, the surrender value is less than the total amount paid for the product for at least a decade, even if the policyholder never has to tap into the "savings fund" for financial emergencies. Insurance experts say any cash value policy would be a poor choice for soldiers trying to maximize the amount their families would receive in the event of their deaths.

"It might very well be good advice to let the low-benefit, high-premium so-called savings program go and stay with the lower-price term insurance," said Joseph M. Belth, emeritus professor of insurance at Indiana University and editor of The Insurance Forum, an independent periodical.

In fact, Private Deuel did keep the $250,000 Military Benefit Association policy he had purchased, according to the agents who sold it to him, and canceled the more expensive Trans World policy, a choice that most financial experts would have endorsed.

Mr. Worsham also cited the case of Pvt. Marlin T. Rockhold, 23, killed by a sniper in Baghdad in May 2003, leaving a wife and her 9-year-old daughter at Fort Stewart, in Hinesville, Ga. At his death, the young private had $250,000 in military insurance, shared equally by his wife and his mother.

But eight months earlier, he had applied to buy $272,000 in additional insurance from one of Mr. Worsham's agents in Hinesville. According to the local agent, Private Rockhold canceled his application three days later, saying a noncommissioned officer at the base had told him he did not need additional insurance.

Like Private Deuel, Private Rockhold had signed up for the two types of insurance -- but unlike Private Deuel, he had canceled both policies, even the low-cost one through the Military Benefit Association that would have given him $250,000 in supplemental coverage for $18.75 a month, with the entire amount going to his widow.

The other policy he canceled was a Flexible Dollar Builder from the American Fidelity Life Insurance Company in Pensacola, Fla., a sister company to Trans World. That policy would have cost Private Rockhold $60 a month for a death benefit of $22,000. Under the terms of the policy, he would not have accumulated any savings in the first year to supplement the stated death benefit, according to the documentation supplied by Mr. Worsham.

Two other soldiers on Mr. Worsham's list had also applied for both types of insurance, sold in tandem, and had also subsequently canceled both policies.

One, Pvt. Kevin C. Ott, who died in Iraq last June, had applied for just $50,000 of term insurance from the Military Benefit Association at a cost of $3.75 a month. He had also signed up for $25,000 of Flexible Dollar Builder insurance from American Fidelity for $100 a month, but had arranged to contribute an additional amount each month to the policy's accumulation fund, for a total monthly deduction of more than $158 for the second policy. Thus, he would have spent almost $162 a month for death benefits of $75,000, plus the money he paid into the second policy's savings fund before his death.

The other soldier, Pvt. Joseph Favorito 3rd, who died in a training accident in Louisiana in late 2002, had also signed up for $50,000 in low-cost Military Benefit Association coverage for $3.75 a month. His American Fidelity policy would have given him $26,000 in additional coverage, but would have cost $60 a month, none of which would have been paid into his accumulation fund in the first year.

The fifth soldier cited by Mr. Worsham was Sgt. Troy D. Jenkins of the Army, who was mortally wounded in April 2003 when he threw himself on an unexploded cluster bomb that had been brought to a group of soldiers by an Iraqi child. Sergeant Jenkins left a wife and two young children, according to military news releases.

The insurance agency that dealt with Sergeant Jenkins at Fort Campbell, Ky., sells both the low-cost Military Benefit Association term insurance, which would have provided up to $250,000 in additional benefits for his young family, and the Flexible Dollar Builder product. But according to the documents provided by Mr. Worsham, Sergeant Jenkins had applied in October 2002 for only the more expensive policy from American Fidelity, which provided $27,500 in coverage for $100 a month -- and listed a friend as the primary beneficiary.

Sergeant Jenkins later canceled that policy, saying he was acting on the advice of his "chain of command," according to a letter from the local agent.

The complexities in the five cases illustrate the challenges that confront the G.A.O. study team. Mr. Worsham said that he had shipped 6,000 unconsummated insurance applications to the G.A.O. for its review, and he estimated that half of them were applications that soldiers filled out but subsequently withdrew, saying they were acting on the advice of senior officers. The other half, he said, were applications for policies that had not gone into effect because military finance offices had not processed the paperwork that would allow the soldiers to have their premiums automatically deducted from their paychecks.

Among the cases are some submitted by R. Lee Brown, a retired command sergeant major who sells insurance near Fort Hood, Tex. Mr. Brown, in a telephone interview last week, said about 50 soldiers filled out applications to buy insurance from him in March, just before they shipped out to Iraq. But so far, he said, none of their payroll deduction paperwork has been processed, leaving them without the additional insurance coverage they wanted.

The delayed paperwork may be an administrative lapse, but Mr. Worsham said he and Mr. Brown suspect that the payroll-deduction paperwork was simply "trashed" by finance officers who thought that the insurance the soldiers wanted to purchase was unnecessary. Pentagon officials have said that any military personnel found to have improperly interfered with a soldier's well-informed decision to buy supplemental insurance will be punished.

Mr. Worsham rejected the idea that officers who may have advised their troops to cancel policies may not have understood that there are some supplemental policies worth keeping, even if others are far less suitable.

Instead, he argued that many in the military establishment are prejudiced against American Fidelity and Trans World, the two companies that sell the Flexible Dollar Builder. In the late 1990's both companies and some of their agents were temporarily barred from several military bases after investigations confirmed that they had violated Pentagon rules governing the sale of insurance on military bases. Both were also sued in the late 1990's over their business practices by the Justice Department and by Florida insurance regulators; they settled both cases without admitting any wrongdoing.

URL: http://www.nytimes.com

GRAPHIC: Photos: Michael R. Deuel canceled some of his life insurance coverage before going to Iraq. (pg. C1)
Troy D. Jenkins, left, Marlin T. Rockhold and Kevin C. Ott are among those some life insurers have offered as proof that soldiers are being prevented from getting some insurance coverage before going abroad. (Photographs by Associated Press)
Richard L. Worsham oversees over 150 insurance agents serving military bases in eight states. He lobbied for the G.A.O. investigation. (Photo by Christopher Berkey for The New York Times)(pg. C4)

The New York Times September 2, 2004 Thursday

The New York Times

September 2, 2004 Thursday
Late Edition - Final

SECTION: Section C; Column 5; Business/Financial Desk; Pg. 1

LENGTH: 1233 words

HEADLINE: Congress Puts Insurance Sales To Military Under Scrutiny

BYLINE: By DIANA B. HENRIQUES

BODY:

State and federal investigators and members of Congress are broadening their efforts to address problems in the sale of life insurance and mutual funds to young soldiers and other service members on military installations nationwide.

A Georgia congressman has drafted legislation aimed at preventing marketing practices that have exposed young recruits to high-pressure or misleading sales pitches for products that may not fit their financial needs, and a prominent lawmaker said yesterday that a House subcommittee would hold a hearing on the issue next Thursday.

Spurred by growing Congressional interest, the Government Accountability Office is expanding a study of military insurance sales that it began last spring, an official at the agency said this week.

And insurance regulators in at least two states -- Georgia and Texas -- have started examinations of insurance sales on military bases under their jurisdiction.

Of these initiatives, the most potentially far-reaching one is a bill proposed by Representative Max Burns, a Georgia Republican whose legislative district includes several large military installations, including Fort Stewart and Fort Gordon.

The bill, which Mr. Burns said he would file when Congress reconvenes on Tuesday, would amend federal securities laws to ban the sale of contractual plans, an obscure type of mutual fund widely marketed on military bases. The plans, common in the fund industry until the 1970's but virtually obsolete in the civilian market today, impose sales charges that consume 50 percent of an investor's first-year contributions. "It is an outrage that financial products that were found so disreputable that they disappeared from the civilian market 20 years ago have continued to survive on post," said Mr. Burns, an Army veteran and former college professor.

His bill would also strengthen the hand of state regulators in policing insurance sales abuses on military bases and give each state's insurance commissioner a year to establish standards to protect service members on military installations from predatory practices.

"We cannot allow those who defend our freedom to continue to be unfairly targeted for the sale of dubious financial products," said Mr. Burns, who was in New York City yesterday for the Republican National Convention. "I've asked that the House Committee on Financial

Services arrange expedited hearings."

His wish was granted yesterday afternoon when the office of Representative Michael G. Oxley, the committee's chairman, announced that a hearing would be held at 10 a.m. next Thursday on the broad topic of "G.I. Finances: Protecting Those Who Protect Us."

Mr. Oxley said yesterday: "Military personnel have special needs when it comes to financial products. Their lives are at risk, and many are young with growing families."

The hearing will be conducted by his panel's subcommittee on capital markets, insurance and government-sponsored enterprises, whose chairman is Representative Richard H. Baker, Republican of Louisiana.

If enacted, Mr. Burns's bill would have a substantial effect on the business of First Command Financial Planning in Fort Worth, which has sold hundreds of thousands of these investment plans to young service men and women around the world.

But Paul Cozby, a spokesman for First Command, said the company would support and comply with whatever changes Congress decided to make in the law governing contractual plans. "In fact, we have discussed with Mr. Burns some of these changes and have offered ideas for industry improvements," Mr. Cozby said. He added, "We hope that any changes enacted by Congress will protect people who are currently invested in contractual plans."

The G.A.O.'s study of military insurance sales was begun in March at the request of four House members who had received industry complaints that military personnel were mishandling the paperwork submitted by soldiers seeking to buy supplemental insurance before being deployed to Iraq and other dangerous places.

Derek Stewart, the director of military and civilian personnel issues at the G.A.O., said this week that Congressional interest in the project had boomed since July, with at least a half-dozen additional members adding their names to the original list of lawmakers requesting the study.

And rather than focusing just on the paperwork problems cited by the industry last spring, Mr. Stewart said, the study will explore "the whole process: how is supplemental insurance coverage being accomplished? How expensive is it? Are the companies scrupulously going about their business?"

The agency has already made investigative visits to several bases, Mr. Stewart said, and visits to others may be scheduled, given the widening interest on Capitol Hill.

"My team is taking in new information every day," Mr. Stewart said. He declined to disclose the contents of a preliminary briefing his team gave to Congressional staff members, but he said, "There are problems here, definitely." He said he hoped to release a public report by February.

At the state level, an investigation has been initiated by John W. Oxendine, the chief insurance regulator in Georgia, which has one of the nation's highest concentrations of military bases. "This is a very high-level investigation," Mr. Oxendine said. "We take this extremely seriously."

Mr. Oxendine and Representative Burns both said their initiatives were prompted by articles in The New York Times in July that described how some financial companies had used misleading or improper sales tactics to sell to military consumers, or had promoted products -- like high-cost life insurance and contractual plans -- that were ill suited to their financial needs.

Mr. Oxendine said his staff had contacted legal officers at every military installation in the state and, after some early mixed results, was now getting "a high level of cooperation." In the next few weeks, his investigators will take sworn statements from some service members who may have been misled about their insurance purchases, he said.

His staff also plans to conduct an on-site examination this week at the home office of the American Amicable Life Insurance Company in Waco, Tex., he said, and investigators are examining the files of several Georgia insurance agencies, including some in Columbus, the home of Fort Benning.

Lanny Peavy, the president and chief executive of American Amicable, said yesterday that his company had taken remedial steps in response to complaints about the improper sale of its policies at two major military bases in recent years and was cooperating fully with Mr. Oxendine's examination and with Congressional inquiries.

"Our desire is to responsibly respond to inquiries while continuing to provide solid, stable insurance products to our customers," Mr. Peavy said.

In response to Georgia's action, insurance regulators in Texas have opened a preliminary inquiry as well, said Jerry Hagins, a spokesman for the Texas Department of Insurance. He said there had been "no developments to report so far."

Mr. Oxendine said he intended to discuss his concerns with other state insurance regulators at the annual meeting of the National Association of Insurance Commissioners, to be held next weekend in Anchorage. "I want to raise the question of whether we should take some sort of multistate action in this area," he said.

Senator CLINTON. Thank you.

Often these agents were able to get on bases with the tacit approval of base commanders and often the insurance companies employed retired military officers who conveyed a real sense of authority. The servicemembers were convinced to sign up for policies that required large payments to be taken out of their paychecks.

Last Congress, Senator Enzi and I introduced legislation to ban periodic payment plans which were the most egregious of these policies and to require better recordkeeping and a registry of unscrupulous agents. Our companion legislation did pass Congress before adjournment. We plan to reintroduce that legislation this Congress, and I would commend that both to the committee and also to our witnesses because I think it is an important piece of the puzzle. If the insurance is going to be available, then we owe it to the servicemembers and their families that it be insurance of the highest integrity.

Another piece of this is the financial education issue. I think that this is a concern because, although there are programs which you have discussed which educate some of our servicemembers about insurance policies, about car insurance, and the like, it is important that we make sure we have uniform education across all Services and all bases because from our checking on this, it is quite uneven. Some commanders take it more seriously than others. Some feel that if you are old enough to be in the military, look out for yourself. But when you are 17, 18, or 19, there is still a lot to learn. I think that part of our obligation, not only to our servicemembers but to their families, is to make sure that as they are becoming acclimated, getting used to being in the Service, getting, maybe for the first time, used to being away from home, that they are not taken advantage of at the very moment they have signed up to serve our country.

I am also concerned about the payday lending abuses that are going on around our bases, which is another issue that I would like to have included in this overall look that we are taking. Chairman Warner, I would be very interested in working with Senator Collins and looking at this broader range of insurance abuses, payday lending abuses, just so we have a handle on what is going on and what we might do to try to prevent that.

Chairman WARNER. Senator, that will be done. You two are a great team. I am very conscious of that. It is just a continuation of what you have been doing since the first day you joined the committee.

Senator CLINTON. Thank you, Mr. Chairman.

Finally, we have in the audience representatives of the Gold Star Wives of America. I have been privileged to develop a very close working relationship with both the Gold Star Wives and the Gold Star Mothers. With respect to some of these issues that we are asking that you look into, and particularly, Secretary Chu, with respect to the charge that the chairman gave to you, I think it would be useful to include the observations and experiences of the Gold Star Wives and Mothers. Some of the concerns about the casualty assistance officers that have been raised with me by the Gold Star Wives and Mothers really need to be brought to your attention because I think this is a wonderful opportunity to improve what we are already doing and to remedy any of the problems that are seen firsthand by those who are really on the front lines of survivors because they are the ones who receive that knock on the door.

Mr. Chairman, I would ask unanimous consent to submit the statement of the Gold Star Wives of America also for the record.

Senator SESSIONS. Without objection, it will be made a part of the record.

Senator CLINTON. Thank you. Thank you very much, gentlemen.

Senator SESSIONS. Senator DeWine, we are glad to have you with us today.

Senator DEWINE. Mr. Chairman, I want to thank you and Chairman Warner for your graciousness in allowing me, not as a member of the committee, to ask a few questions and take a little of your time. I appreciate it very much.

I agree with the sentiment that has been expressed by many members of the panel and others today about really treating all the families of service men and women who die in service to their country equally. I think it is just so very important.

We are now mourning in Ohio machinist mate second class Joseph Ashley. He died on the U.S.S. *San Francisco.* It ran aground near Guam on January 9. He died in service to our country. Megan Elizabeth Edelman died in a parachute accident. Her services will be this week. It was only her second jump. This was a training exercise here in the United States. Those are just two examples from my home State of Ohio.

Senator McCain gave another example. We can all think of examples. A helicopter goes down in Texas, a training exercise. You cannot distinguish them. They are in service to their country. They sign up. Each life is given so that we can be free and that we can live in peace.

I think that as we go about our business in crafting this legislation, as you do, Mr. Chairman, here in this committee and do such a great job and as we do on the floor, that we should listen to the comments that have been made by the members of this panel today and take that into consideration.

Let me also make another comment that I made earlier today and maybe amplify it a little bit and then ask a question. I think that it is very proper that we raise these benefits, the lump sum benefit. I commend Senator Sessions and others who have done this. They are absolutely correct. It needs to be done, Mr. Chairman.

I still worry, though, about what is going to happen in 15, 16, or 17 years. I think about the little babies, some of them who never saw their father. We have a moral obligation, to see that they, if they want to, get to go to college or get to go to a vocational school, whatever they want to do post-secondary. Whatever they want to do, they ought to have the right to do that. If you look at the amount of money we have set aside today, it is just not quite enough. It just is not there, and we have to change it. To say that we have set aside so much money in a lump sum payment, it is just not the same thing because a lot can happen in 17 years. That is just the way the world works. Our obligation is to the child of the deceased service man or woman. So, Mr. Chairman, we ought to look at that and we have to look at that.

Finally, I want to address the issue of health care. The bill that has been introduced by the leadership does cover this, something I was very concerned about, and I would hope the committee would take that part of that bill at least and incorporate it into whatever bill that you craft. I do want to mention it.

It goes back to something that Dr. Chu said about trying to get some of the same benefits and put these families in the same shape that they were in during the time that the serviceman is alive. During the life of the servicemember, dependents have cost-free access to military health systems, including many services for special needs children. Following the death of the servicemember, the surviving dependents continue to receive military health care free for 3 years, but then, under current law, are subject to yearly enrollment fees and copayments.

It seems to me that it would be helpful, as provided in the leader's bill that was introduced, to the families of deceased servicemembers if we would remove the unnecessary burden and worry of enrollment fees and copayments that can become substantial in the case certainly of a special needs child. That would do exactly what Dr. Chu said, and that would put this family in the same position they would have been in if that servicemember would have lived.

It seems to me, General Cody and others, that is what we ought to try to do. We are not trying to give them something they would not have had, but you cannot bring that mom or dad back, but what we can do, what this compassionate society ought to do, is step in there and say we want to make sure you can go to a State university at least, which is all my bill would do, is to provide enough money to get to go to a State university, room, board, tuition, and provide enough so that the medical is taken care of.

I wonder if any of the servicemembers in uniform would comment on that broad concept without getting into the details, but of the broad concept of trying to do that. General, you are nodding your head there. I always like nodders when they are nodding yes. [Laughter.]

General CODY. Senator, I think you are absolutely right. What we have talked about here today is to take care of the initial, as well as set up the future of the family unit. What needs to be looked at is the potential loss in terms of the young soldier who died at a certain rank. Had he not died, he would have probably retired in 20 years at two or three levels higher, gotten that retirement pay, but still had some more earning potential later, and been able to provide for his family in a different way. So that is the gap that we need to take a look at.

Certainly education, being what it is today, just having paid for two sons going through college, is expensive. We should have something. I do not know if it should be on the back of the Office of the Secretary of Defense or the VA, but as we take a look across this great country and take a look at our universities and everything else, we ought to have some type of means so that they take this up. We give preference at the military academies for those sons and daughters of deceased servicemembers, but that is based on order of merit. There are other things we can do, because I think the education of these family members that are left behind is something we need to pay attention to and it is the most costly.

Senator DEWINE. Well, I appreciate it. My time is up.

Mr. EPLEY. May I add something to that, Senator, from the VA's perspective?

Senator DEWINE. With the chairman's permission, certainly.

Mr. EPLEY. The VA does have benefit programs geared toward the survivors of service men and women who die in service or die from a service-connected disability. It provides for payments currently at $803 a month if the son or daughter is in full-time training, beginning at age 18 through age 26, and it offers up to 45 months of entitlement to that training. We are currently paying about 58,000 of those children, either survivors or children of totally disabled servicemen today. That compares to the Montgomery GI Bill, a benefit for veterans themselves, which is currently $1,004 per month. Congress raised the rate two times in the last year or year and a half. It was about $680 prior to that time. Certainly we need to make sure that it is commensurate with the costs of higher education.

Senator DEWINE. I appreciate it.

Thank you, Mr. Chairman.

Senator SESSIONS. Thank you, Senator DeWine.

Chairman Warner, it is an honor to be with you and to be in the odd position of chairing the chairman. You are too kind and gracious to allow me to do this.

Chairman WARNER. I wanted to be the wrap-up here, and I certainly want to defer to the leaders like yourself on both sides—this is truly a bipartisan issue—that have taken initiatives and I thank you again.

In that vein, I would like to ask unanimous consent that a statement by Senator Hagel—I mentioned him earlier in my opening remarks—be admitted to the record. He was one of the cosponsors.

Senator SESSIONS. We have that and without objection.

[The prepared statement of Senator Hagel follows:]

PREPARED STATEMENT BY SENATOR CHUCK HAGEL

Chairman Warner and Senator Levin, thank you for holding this very important hearing on survivor benefits for our latest generation of warriors who have given their lives in service to our country. This committee makes a clear statement to America about the priorities of our country: our men and women in uniform and their families.

On January 23, the Lincoln Journal Star reported that Nebraska ranks fifth in the number of military deaths per capita in Iraq. In the story, the families of Marine Captain Travis Ford of Ogallala, Marine Corporal Matt Henderson of Lincoln, Army Sergeant Cory Mracek of Hay Springs and Marine Private Noah Boye of Grand Island shared their personal stories of how they have grieved and are struggling to grasp life without their loved one. Their stories are filled with hardship. But they are also filled with a strong will and determination to let the memory and legacy of our soldiers live proudly in their hearts and communities. These stories inspire all of us and make us proud to be Americans.

Last Monday, I reintroduced legislation to raise the military survivor benefit paid to the families of military personnel killed while on Active-Duty from $12,420 to $100,000. The families of our first responders across the Nation receive between $50,000 and $100,000 as a survivor benefit for the loss of their firefighter or police officer. My legislation proposes that this legislation apply retroactively to all servicemembers on Active-Duty who have died after September 11, 2001.

The military death gratuity is money provided immediately to families of our servicemembers who are killed while on Active-Duty. These funds assist next-of-kin with their immediate financial needs. These financial needs and challenges are no different for the families of servicemembers who have lost their lives outside combat zones than they are for those who have died in Iraq or Afghanistan. My legislation therefore increases the military death gratuity for all servicemembers who die while on Active-Duty. This is an issue of fundamental fairness.

As we face the challenges of the 21st century, service men and women sacrificing for their country in a time of war need to be assured that, should the worst occur, their families will be properly provided for. The loss of a loved one is a tremendous emotional hardship for families. Congress should do what it can to ensure that it does not cause extreme financial hardship as well.

Though nothing can replace the hole torn in a family by the loss of a son, daughter, mother, or father, the "Military Death Benefit Improvement Act of 2005" will help alleviate some of the financial hardships faced by the families of our brave service men and women who give their lives in service to our country. It will send a message to our brave young men and women and their families that their Nation appreciates their service and sacrifice. I urge my colleagues on the Armed Services Committee to move swiftly to improve the death benefits paid to the families of the brave men and women who give their lives in service to our great country.

Thank you.

Chairman WARNER. Mr. Epley, we have a marvelous man, Jim Nicholson, who has taken over from Secretary Principi now as the new presidential appointee running your Department. I have known him for a long time. He is a decorated Vietnam veteran and a man in whom I have a lot of confidence and great respect. I would hope that you would give him a full report of this hearing because our committee wants to work in tandem and in partnership with the Veterans' Affairs Committee, and I am sure that he wants to work with Secretary Rumsfeld, Dr. Chu, and others in working this legislation.

We will try and use as a target the legislation going through, as Senator Sessions mentioned, the omnibus bill. These types of legislation, in my long experience on this committee, should be given the highest priority. I think America wants it first and foremost.

It is interesting. The men and women of the Armed Forces who experienced these grievous losses of family and so forth, have come through quietly in their modest ways, but the American public really is behind them to get this legislation. So let us move forward with that.

Before I go a little further here, Dr. Chu, in my opening remarks, I wanted to compliment you on your long service in the Department. I guess you have combined service of more years in presidential appointments than anybody else serving in the Department today. I don't imagine that you spend time sitting down and adding it all up, but it is close to 15-some-odd years or more. Am I not correct?

Dr. CHU. Yes, sir.

Chairman WARNER. Who was that famous person who said the reports of my demise are greatly exagerated or something? I think we had in mind Dr. Feith when we were talking about the early departure. So we will strike from the record your departure.

Dr. CHU. I appreciate that, Senator. I thought maybe you were sending me a message of some kind. [Laughter.]

Chairman WARNER. No, no. If this old chairman is going to send you a message, he just barrels it out in a blunt way. He is not going to do it subtly. Do not worry about that.

Senator LEVIN. Senator Warner, I am afraid I followed your lead again in also thanking Dr. Chu for his service. I have to be more cautious in doing that! But thanks anyway for your service, Dr. Chu. [Laughter.]

Dr. CHU. I appreciate it.

Chairman WARNER. I am going to leave to go out to this dedication of this new rehabilitation center, which we are privileged to have in Virginia. But I want to sort of wrap up with the following.

We have to be mindful, as we move in this legislative package, of the first responders here in America. Certainly they, through their professionalism and the arduous tasks that they perform, be it the police, firemen, or many others, are subjected to high risk of death and injury, as are other members of the armed services. We want to pay them appropriate tribute here in the context of this hearing. I think this legislation moves in a direction that would provide a total package for the men and women of the Armed Forces that is quite different than the packages in the States for the first responders and those in the Federal system. But I think their record has helped contribute here in Congress to the early recognition and consideration of the one for the military. I wanted to mention that.

Now, Dr. Chu, having been in your position for many years—some 35 years ago, I was privileged to be Secretary of the Navy—I know full well there are times when the civilian side of the house has viewpoints which at some times are at variance with the uniformed side. That is the strength of the system, and it should always be that way. It is by no means any criticism. I have found it exceedingly helpful. But the buck does stop on the Secretary of Defense's desk as you send that buck up.

I would like to conclude this hearing this morning, or my participation here in this question period, with asking you to let us define with some precision those differences as we view them as of today, because Congress will move into the vacuum. I want Congress to move into that vacuum and work with the DOD to resolve it or take its own initiatives, but let us do so well informed.

Now, one of them is this issue of the qualification for benefits. The eligible military today, I think quite properly—and I must say I associate my views with them for the moment—should not be limited to personnel in designated geographic areas. Is that one area of difference, Dr. Chu, that needs to be resolved legislatively?

Dr. CHU. I would actually ask to follow the provision in the Sessions, Lieberman, et cetera bill, which leaves that to the discretion of the Secretary. My colleagues here this morning had mentioned line-of-duty as one approach we could take. The thinking we have on this point has two important elements. One, the Nation particularly wants to recognize those who have fallen in Iraq and Afghanistan. Second, we lose service personnel—on I–395 for example, in a variety of peacetime, and nontraining situations. Is that appropriate for this same payment or not, particularly if there is a contribution from the individual to the tragic event? I would urge that discretion be given the Secretary on the point of how we cover this. You might wish to consider report language that guides us in using that discretion as to what your intent is.

Chairman WARNER. All right. Senator Sessions, you will be among those who will be working on this issue. Let us have some precision on that. I believe an element of discretion reposed in the Secretary is a wise piece of legislation to have in there.

Would a second one be the date of retroactivity, or are we pretty much in agreement?

Dr. CHU. I think we all agree it should be October 7, 2001. That is the start of combat operations in Afghanistan.

Chairman WARNER. Now, are there any others that come to mind, any other areas where there could be at the moment some difference of views between the civilian side of the house and the uniformed side?

Dr. CHU. The other important point that I am aware of is how one consults with the next of kin on a declination of insurance. Again, I think we leave some discretion to the Secretary as to how that happens. I think it is very helpful, and Senator Sessions' and Senator Lieberman's bill calls out the need to do something here, just as you have guided us on this point in the SBP legislation much earlier.

Chairman WARNER. All right.

Our distinguished acting chairman, can you think of any other differences that come to mind here before we close out?

Senator SESSIONS. No. Other than the additional suggestions such as from Senator DeWine on health care benefits or education interests, I do not know of any other specific items that need to be settled. I think the Veterans Committee suggested $300,000, as the increase from $250,000 to $300,000 rather than to $400,000. So that is a matter that we may need to think through.

Chairman WARNER. Well, that is within the Veterans' Affairs jurisdiction. We want to be very careful to coordinate with their jurisdictional responsibilities.

Well, then that concludes my comments on this, colleagues and our distinguished witness panel. I thank all of you. You have done a great service to those on Active-Duty and to their families and others, as you have come up forthrightly in your testimony today, and I am confident that Congress will act swiftly. I compliment the Department, Dr. Chu, through your good efforts and those of the Secretary and the Deputy Secretary.

Dr. CHU. Thank you, sir.

Chairman WARNER. Thank you very much. I entrust this to you and Senator Levin.

Senator SESSIONS. Thank you.

Chairman WARNER. Again, I thank Senator Levin for his leadership on this issue, not only on this but on many others. But you have your own bill, and I presume that the area in which we are moving is consistent with the objectives and goals that you had in mind, Senator Levin?

Senator LEVIN. Trying to eliminate that distinction is an important goal, and we do eliminate the distinction as to where the death took place in our bill.

Chairman WARNER. Good. I thank you.

Senator LEVIN. One other area that is complicated, it seems to me, is that the proposal I believe the administration is supporting suggests that the extra insurance will be provided in the event that the death occurs in the AO and that the premium will be paid for.

Dr. CHU. No, sir. What we are supporting, as I think has been outlined this morning, is an increase in SGLI for everybody to $400,000.

Senator LEVIN. Right.

Dr. CHU. In addition, we would like a provision, which I think is parallel to the Sessions-Lieberman bill provision, that would allow us to finance that for everyone in the AO designated by the Secretary. The intent there is to ensure that everyone, notwithstanding whatever next-of-kin provision we work out, is afforded some level of insurance, even if they declined. So if you selected the full $400,000, you would get a rebate on your premium. You would get a lower premium basically. If you did not, we would buy the insurance for you anyway.

Senator LEVIN. I just would raise the administrative complexity about having the premium——

Dr. CHU. We are discussing that with the VA. Compared to commercial policies, I think this is relatively straightforward frankly.

Senator LEVIN. Well, it is not straightforward if, when you are in the AO, you get a premium paid for what you do not get if you are outside of the AO.

Dr. CHU. We have a whole series of pays, as you are aware, Senator, that are triggered by AO constraints.

Senator LEVIN. I just want to raise that issue.

Dr. CHU. We think it is tractable.

Senator LEVIN. Okay.

The other issue that I have has to do with the legislation, Dr. Chu, which we enacted giving the DOD and other Federal agencies a requirement that senior executives be paid on the basis of performance.

Now, you issued a memorandum. You signed a memorandum on January 12 saying to all of the Secretaries that you may not grant an across-the-board increase to Senior Executive Service (SES) members. You may not grant an across-the-board increase. Yet, we find that an across-the-board increase has been now ordered for political appointees.

Dr. CHU. You are speaking, I think, to Mr. DuBois' memorandum regarding Washington Headquarters Services. Is that correct?

Senator LEVIN. Yes.

Dr. CHU. That is not quite accurate. My understanding is that they still have to demonstrate a fully successful performance.

Senator LEVIN. Yes, but fully-successful level is the lowest level. Right?

Dr. CHU. No. There is unsuccessful, basically.

Senator LEVIN. Well, what about career SES members performing at the fully-successful level? Are they guaranteed that pay?

Dr. CHU. Let me step back from the specifics of his memo and outline the process we tried to put in place. We tried to encourage each major component of the Department, the three military departments, and then what some like to call the fourth estate, to craft within the parameters of the statute a performance-oriented result. Now, from my memorandum, I set the standard that you could not just give everybody the same thing and that your decisions need to have a performance foundation. I left each component to its discretion how it could best carry that out.

Senator LEVIN. Now, noncareer SES members that perform at the fully-successful level will receive an increase of 2.5 percent. Is that correct? That is what the decision was.

Dr. CHU. That is Mr. DuBois' choice for the Washington career service. Yes, sir, that is correct.

Senator LEVIN. Is that true for career SES members?

Dr. CHU. No, he set a different standard for those reflecting——

Senator LEVIN. I think that is inconsistent with our statute and with your memo because he is treating career and noncareer SES folks differently. All the fully-successful are better——

Dr. CHU. Can I make a suggestion, sir? Let me get him to come up and explain——

Senator LEVIN. No, no. I want you to tell me whether you believe that his memo, which distinguishes between career and noncareer SES members, is consistent with your memo. That is what I want.

Dr. CHU. I think it is consistent because he set a performance standard. Whether it is consistent with the statute, I leave to the general counsel who tries to review these things for me and make sure I am on the right path in each case. But to the philosophy that is involved, his argument for this choice is that the noncareer SES received actually in the previous round a smaller increase. So he is trying to look on a multi-year basis as to how was this done.

Senator LEVIN. Regardless of what his motive or purpose is—and that is arguable—the law says that we have to treat the career and noncareer SES folks the same. He has distinguished between them by saying that if you have fully-successful performance or better, you get a 2.5 percent pay raise.

Dr. CHU. I am delighted to go back to my legal counsel and make sure we are in the right place in allowing him to do this.

Senator LEVIN. Was it the legal counsel who wrote your memo?

Dr. CHU. We wrote the memo and we asked them to review it.

Senator LEVIN. All right.

Mr. Chairman, with your permission, could we ask the legal counsel whether or not distinguishing between career and non-career the way that we have just described is consistent with our statute which says we cannot distinguish between career and non-career, that performance-based compensation is what we required? So that would be the question which would be asked. With your permission, I would like to ask that——

Senator SESSIONS. We will leave the hearing open for questions, and you will be able to submit that. I would suggest that that would be a good approach.

Senator LEVIN. Thank you, Dr. Chu, and thank you, Mr. Chairman.

Senator SESSIONS. Gentlemen, thank you for your testimony today and for your service to your country. I think there is a good feeling out there among the American people about doing more for families who have lost a loved one in combat. It has been surprising to me the groundswell of grassroots support that have come to my office and others who have been talking about this issue. People want to be generous to those who serve. We thank you for your excellent testimony today.

I would offer for the record a letter from the American Legion, the Veterans of Foreign Wars, and the Disabled American Veterans, which specifically have endorsed the HEROES Act that Senator Lieberman and I have offered, although all of us are moving in a bipartisan, collegial way to develop the best language that we can come up with in that regard.

[The letter from the American Legion, the Veterans of Foreign Wars, and the Disabled American Veterans follows:]

The American Legion

For God and Country

★ WASHINGTON OFFICE ★ 1608 "K" STREET, N.W. ★ WASHINGTON, D.C. 20006-2847 ★
(202) 861-2700 ★

January 25, 2005

The Honorable Jeff Sessions
335 Russell Senate Office Building
United States Senate
Washington, D.C. 20510-0104

Dear Senator Sessions:

On behalf of the 2.8 million members of The American Legion, I would like to express our full support for the Honoring Every Requirement of Exemplary Act of 2005/HEROES Act of 2005. The initiatives outlined in this bill will greatly assist the their families and loved ones of servicemen and women who died in combat.

The American Legion supports the augmentation of the lump-sum death benefit and the maximum payout from life insurance to families of soldiers killed in combat. For those who have made the ultimate sacrifice in defense of our freedoms, this act goes far to ease the hardships incurred by those families. However, The American Legion believes the benefits of this act should be extended to the families of all our servicemen and women killed in the service of the nation.

Once again, The American Legion fully supports Honoring Every Requirement of Exemplary Act of 2005/HEROES Act of 2005. The American Legion appreciates your continued leadership in addressing the issues that are important to veterans, members of the Armed Forces and their families.

Sincerely,

Steve A. Robertson, Director
National Legislative Commission

VETERANS OF FOREIGN WARS

OF THE UNITED STATES

January 24, 2005

The Honorable Jeff Sessions
335 Russell Senate Office Building
United States Senate
Washington, D.C. 20510

Dear Senator Sessions:

On behalf of the 2.4 million members of the Veterans of Foreign Wars of the United States and our Ladies Auxiliary, I would like to offer our support for "*The HEROES Act of 2005,*" legislation that would amend Title 10 and Title 38, United States Code, to improve benefits for the families of deceased members of the Armed Forces.

As the number of servicemen and women killed in the war on terror continues, it is imperative that we recognize the need to provide not only emotional support to their families, but much-needed financial assistance during this troubling time.

By increasing the current $12,000 military death gratuity payment to $100,000, your legislation will stand by the Federal government's promise to take care of those left behind when a servicemember dies in the line of duty. We also applaud the bill's proposal that would increase the Servicemembers Group Life Insurance (SGLI) maximum benefit from $250,000 to $400,000. VFW resolution 642, passed at our National Convention in August, calls for legislation to improve the SGLI benefit; an increase we believe is long overdue.

Once again, thank you for introducing legislation that will help ensure that those families that have lost a loved one in the name of freedom receive the support and financial assistance that truly demonstrates our appreciation for those who sacrificed all.

We look forward to working with you and your staff on this legislation. As always, thank you for your continued support of America's veterans.

Sincerely,

Dennis Cullinan
National Legislative Service

CC: Senator Joseph Lieberman
Attachments (1) VFW Resolution 642

DAV DISABLED AMERICAN VETERANS
Building Better Lives for America's Disabled Veterans

January 27, 2005

The Honorable Jeff Sessions
United States Senate
335 Russell Senate Office Building
Washington, DC 20515

Dear Senator Sessions:

This will acknowledge receipt of your letter requesting endorsement of S.77, which would improve death benefits for the families of deceased members of the Armed Forces by increasing military death gratuity from $12,000 to $100,000, and enhancing Servicemembers Group Life Insurance.

The Disabled American Veterans (DAV) agrees that survivors of servicemembers killed in action suffer great financial hardships and deserve adequate recompense. Therefore, we fully support S.77 and your efforts to improve the lives of the survivors of active duty servicemembers.

Thank you for taking the time to write. We appreciate the opportunity to provide our position on this legislation.

Sincerely,

Joseph A. Violante

JOSEPH A. VIOLANTE
National Legislative Director

JAV:lmb

Senator SESSIONS. I would also note that in our last defense authorization bill, I worked with the committee and Chairman Warner and others, and language was put in that bill to require a study of disability benefits for those who are wounded. It would call for the Department to identify and assess the changes in the DOD personnel policies needed to enhance the financial and nonfinancial benefits. It calls on the DOD to consult with the Veterans' Affairs agency, the Veterans Disability Benefit Commission, and it would be finished and completed not more than 150 days from the date of the bill. So, Dr. Chu, that time is running on us.

Dr. CHU. We know the clock is ticking, yes, sir. But it is important, I think, for us to take a fresh review, as Senator McCain and others said. Where are we? What can we do to modernize this in a way that is effective?

Senator SESSIONS. I also appreciate the financial counseling, General Cody, you mentioned, that is provided for young soldiers. We have discussed whether that should be a part of any legislation with regard to families or widows or surviving spouses who lost a loved one and they receive $400,000, $500,000 in payment. I am sure that it will be offered to them. Is that correct, gentlemen? I see you are nodding yes. Through the service support or the Office of the Judge Advocate General, you will be able to provide counseling to them on that. I do not know whether it should be mandatory and some formal procedure set up for that. Perhaps not. I would look forward to your suggestions on that.

If there is no additional business to come before the committee, I will again thank you for you participation today and note that we are adjourned.

[Questions for the record with answers supplied follow:]

QUESTIONS SUBMITTED BY SENATOR PAT ROBERTS

IRS TREATMENT OF DIFFERENTIAL PAY PROVIDED TO MEMBERS OF THE GUARD AND RESERVE

1. Senator ROBERTS. General Cody, Admiral Nathman, General Nyland, and General Moseley, are you aware of any interagency strategy to encourage the Internal Revenue Service (IRS) along and get them to do the right thing by our men and women of the Guard and Reserve?

General CODY. There is no interagency strategy to engage the IRS on behalf of Guard and Reserve members.

Admiral NATHMAN. There is no interagency strategy to engage the IRS on behalf of the Guard and Reserve members.

General NYLAND. According to the IRS, differential pay is not compensation for the recipients since it is not paid for services performed in the employment of companies who voluntarily make such payments. For that reason, payments for differential pay are not "wages" as defined by law under the Internal Revenue Code and are not subject to the taxes imposed by the Federal Insurance Contributions Act and the Federal Unemployment Tax Act or to the Collection of Income Tax at the Source of Wages. Taxpayers must include differential pay in income for Federal tax purposes; however, there is no requirement for employers to withhold income tax from differential pay. Bottom line: There is no interagency strategy to encourage the IRS to alter its guidance on differential pay since the IRS must treat differential pay within the legislative parameters established by the Internal Revenue Code and other applicable laws.

General MOSELEY. Military differential pay is made voluntarily by an employer to represent the difference between the regular salary of an employee called to military Active-Duty and the amount being paid by the military, if the regular salary is higher.

The employment relationship between the employee and the company is interrupted when the worker is called for active military service with the U.S. Government or National Guard. Therefore these payments are not "wages" subject to the taxes imposed by the Federal Insurance Contributions Act and the Federal Unemployment Tax Act or to the Collection of Income Tax at Source on Wages (IRS Revenue Ruling 69–136).

The activated member's employer does not withhold taxes for military differential pay.

The payments are considered income but not "wages" subject to withholding. Therefore, the recipient should prepare for the tax liability by making quarterly estimated tax payments.

Currently the best IRS option for a deployed military member is for that taxpayer to sign up for the Electronic Federal Tax Payment System. This enables the person to schedule payments directly from a bank account for up to a year in advance. It is an easy way for both the taxpayer and the government, and ensures prompt and accurate crediting of payments to the taxpayers account. Other options are for the member to make credit card payments or to send checks with Form 1040–ES vouchers.

Ref: IRS Publication 505, Tax Withholding and Estimated Tax.

2. Senator ROBERTS. General Cody, Admiral Nathman, General Nyland, and General Moseley, has the IRS provided the necessary resources to our troops and their families to ensure that between fighting insurgents and rebuilding a nation, our troops can file their quarterly estimated tax returns if they are able?

General CODY. Yes. In cases where there is no requirement for private employers to withhold income tax from differential pay (pay by a private employer to represent the difference between the employees' regular salary and military pay) the IRS recommends that military members make quarterly estimated tax payments. While there is no legal requirement for recipients of differential pay to pay quarterly estimated taxes, those who choose to pay them may pay by electronic payment (scheduled up to a year in advance), credit card, or check.

As a Department of Defense (DOD) participant in the IRS Volunteer Income Tax Assistance Program, the Army assists soldiers by preparing and filing tax returns. These services extend to soldiers deployed worldwide to include those in combat zones and qualified hazardous duty areas. In addition, current law grants an automatic extension to members of the Armed Forces deployed to combat zones and qualified hazardous duty areas. The automatic extension lasts for a minimum of 180 days after the member returns from deployment to these locations and covers activities such as filing tax returns, paying taxes, and filing claims for a refund.

Admiral NATHMAN, General NYLAND, and General MOSELEY. There is no legal requirement for recipients of differential pay to file quarterly estimated taxes, however this filing approach is one method for those taxpayers to avoid owing the tax all at once when they file their returns. Available options for payment of quarterly estimated taxes include by electronic payment scheduled up to a year in advance, credit card payments or payments by check. Through a partnership with the IRS, the Department of the Navy has an active Volunteer Income Tax Assistance program to aid servicemembers, including those deployed around the world, in completing and filing their tax returns. There are understandable limits on the capability of service personnel deployed to certain geographic locations to complete and file tax returns. Therefore the law grants an automatic extension for filing tax returns, paying taxes, filing claims for refund and taking other actions with IRS for service personnel deployed to a combat zone, qualified hazardous duty area or participating in a qualified contingency operation. The automatic extension lasts for a minimum of 6 months after the individual returns from deployment to such a location.

QUESTIONS SUBMITTED BY SENATOR CARL LEVIN

PAY RAISES FOR POLITICAL APPOINTEES AND CAREER EMPLOYEES

3. Senator LEVIN. Dr. Chu, Section 1125 of the National Defense Authorization Act for Fiscal Year 2004 eliminated the established system for paying senior executives and required the DOD and other Federal agencies to pay senior executives "based on individual performance, contribution to the agency's performance, or both, as determined under a rigorous performance management system." On January 12, 2005, you implemented this provision for the DOD by issuing a memorandum directing the military departments and defense agencies to award pay increases for senior executives "based on their relative standing." Your memorandum expressly prohibited the use of across-the-board increases.

On the same day, however, the Director of Administration and Management for the Office of the Secretary of Defense (OSD) directed an across-the-board pay raise of 2.5 percent—the maximum pay raise allowable—for all senior executives in OSD and the defense agencies who are political appointees and who receive a fully satisfactory rating. By contrast, career civil servants who receive the same rating would be evaluated on their individual performance and contribution to the agency, and only the top performers would receive a 2.5 percent pay raise.

Do you believe that an across-the-board pay raise of 2.5 percent for senior executives in OSD and the defense agencies who are political appointees is consistent with the statutory requirement that pay be "based on individual performance, contribution to the agency's performance, or both, as determined under a rigorous performance management system"?

Dr. CHU. On January 12, 2004, I issued policy regarding SES pay increases. Each DOD component applied that policy based upon its existing pay and performance system, all of which pre-date the new SES pay-for-performance law and regulations. The existing performance management system for executives in OSD and Defense agencies is a three-level rating system, the highest of which is fully successful. Career employees are further evaluated by a performance review board and awards are granted accordingly. Because non-career SES in DODare not eligible for awards, their performance was not subject to review by the performance review board; therefore no further ranking was made under the criteria in place for the most recent performance cycle. Based on those criteria, the decision to increase the pay of non-career and career executives in OSD was based not on status but on performance and contribution as required by law and policy. While the existing system cannot be certified under the current OPM rules, the Department made appropriate decisions regarding the 2005 pay increase. Accordingly, this should not be treated as an example of the new SES pay for performance system, simply because the system has not yet been approved for implementation.

The Department is working closely with the Office of Personnel Management (OPM) on a new SES pay and performance system that will produce positive results and meet the new legal and regulatory requirements necessary for OPM and the Office of Management and Budget certification.

4. Senator LEVIN. Dr. Chu, have you obtained a written opinion from counsel on this issue? If so, please provide a copy of the opinion to the committee. If not, please obtain such an opinion and provide a copy to the committee.

Dr. CHU. Response pending from the Office of General Counsel.

5. Senator LEVIN. Dr. Chu, doesn't the decision to award the maximum allowable pay raise to all political appointees in OSD and the defense agencies undermine DOD's credibility when you say that the new authority granted by the National Security Personnel System (NSPS) will be implemented in a manner that fairly relates pay to performance without bias or favoritism?

Dr. CHU. No. As explained in response to question three, each DOD component based the 2005 pay increase on ratings made under its existing pay and performance system, all of which pre-date the new SES pay-for-performance law and regulations.

The new Executive and Senior Professional Pay and Performance system that we submitted to the Office of Personnel Management for approval contains safeguards to effectively support and meet all legal and regulatory requirements. I can assure you the new system will alleviate your concerns. The new DOD pay system will be credible not only with senior executives but also with other employees who will be entering pay-for-performance systems under the National Security Personnel System.

I am confident that as you look at the Department's new system you will agree that it is both consistent with the requirements of section 1125 of the National Defense Authorization Act for Fiscal Year 2004 and in the best interests of the DOD and its employees.

QUESTIONS SUBMITTED BY SENATOR EDWARD M. KENNEDY

DEATH BENEFITS AND SERVICES AVAILABLE TO SURVIVORS OF MILITARY PERSONNEL

6 and 7. Senator KENNEDY. General Cody, a constituent of mine, Private First Class John Hart from Bedford, Massachusetts, was killed in action in Iraq in October 2003. Before he deployed, he filled out a will along with the other soldiers in his unit. After he was killed, neither the Hart family or the Army could locate his will amongst his personal effects. His family asked the Army to search his personal effects for the will and it was never found. Private Hart's family finally had to declare a lost will and went through Probate in Massachusetts. This painstaking evolution takes both time, money and an attorney, something that nobody that is grieving needs to be exposed, especially when their loved one dies defending our values. What is the procedure for the U.S. Army when it pertains to holding the wills for deploying soldiers? Does the Army hold wills? If not, why?

General CODY. No, the Army does not hold wills. When a will is prepared for a soldier, the soldier is advised of the legal significance of the document and the need to safeguard it. Soldiers are advised to inform their personal representative of the location of the current will and the need to update it after a major life event occurs. In the rare instance when a will is prepared immediately prior to deployment, arrangements are made to mail the will to the soldier's personal representative.

The Army consistently strives to ensure that soldiers are educated regarding the importance of safeguarding their wills and informing the personal representative of the location of the current will. The constant mobility of our soldier-clients and soldier-attorneys and the personal nature of such documents make it impractical for legal assistance offices to be a repository of the wills prepared for soldiers, thus the emphasis on sending the will to the personal representative.

8. Senator KENNEDY. General Cody, I have heard of cases where the personal effects of a person wounded or killed in action are not being returned to them or their loved ones. That certainly was the case with the family of Private John Hart, who was killed in Iraq in October 2003. Please explain the procedures for returning personal effects to loved ones after a servicemember is killed in action.

General CODY. The unit commander is responsible for collecting and evacuating the deceased soldier's personal effects through mortuary affairs channels within the theater of operations to the Joint Personal Effects Depot at Aberdeen Proving Ground, Maryland. The depot will photograph, clean, and inventory the personal effects and then FedEx the deceased soldier's property to the Casualty Assistance Officer (CAO) for delivery to the family. Unfortunately, in the case of Private First Class John Hart, the unit shipped his personal effects directly to his family instead of using mortuary affairs channels. According to the CAO, Mr. and Mrs. Hart received Private First Class Hart's personal effects January 2004. Since this time, we have continued to publish guidance informing our deployed units of the appropriate channels for evacuating the personal effects of deceased and wounded soldiers. Within the past 6 months, we have been able to account for every deceased soldier's personal effects as units comply with established policies and procedures.

QUESTION SUBMITTED BY SENATOR MARK DAYTON

GOVERNMENT HOUSING FOR A SURVIVING MILITARY FAMILY

9. Senator DAYTON. General Cody, Admiral Nathman, General Nyland, and General Moseley, in response to a previous question of mine, each of the Vice Chiefs indicated that base commanders have authority to extend the 6 months that a surviving family can remain in government housing. I know that the first 6 months is at no cost to the family. If this time is extended so that children can complete the school year, or for other reasons, does the family have to pay rent?

General CODY. Yes. When exceptions are submitted and approved by the installation commander for the family to retain housing for an additional 180 days, rent is charged at an amount equal to the Soldier's Basic Allowance for Housing (BAH).

Admiral NATHMAN. Yes. In compliance with the National Defense Authorization Act and Department of Defense Housing Management regulations, surviving family members occupying family housing are allowed to occupy housing without charge for a period of 180 days. The installation commander may extend occupancy beyond the 180 days. When an extension beyond the 180 days is granted, rental rates equivalent to the member's full housing allowances or fair market value of the quarters will be charged.

General NYLAND. In accordance with the DOD Financial Management Regulation (DODFMR), Volume 7A, Table 26–9, rule 19, if family members are residing in government quarters, then the widow/widower (dependents) entitlement to receive BAH exists for 180 days.

In compliance with DOD 4165.63M guidance, family members shall pay a rental rate to continue to remain in family housing. This is after the 180-day period and upon termination of the BAH entitlement.

General MOSELEY. Survivors of military members may stay in government housing longer than 6 months. Survivors would pay rent at fair market rate for any time longer than 6 months.

[Whereupon, at 12:36 p.m., the committee adjourned.]

○

APEX
TP
9780160759093
76901953 – 68